garden
color

Better Homes and Gardens®

garden
color

Better Homes and Gardens® Books
Des Moines, Iowa

Better Homes and Gardens® Books
An imprint of Meredith® Books

Garden Color
Writer: Kathleen Pyle
Editor and Project Manager: Kate Carter Frederick
Art Director: Lyne Neymeyer
Project Coordinator: Beth Ann Edwards
Photo Coordinator: Becky Hendrix
Copy Chief: Terri Fredrickson
Copy and Production Editor: Victoria Forlini
Editorial Operations Manager: Karen Schirm
Managers, Book Production: Pam Kvitne, Marjorie J. Schenkelberg
Contributing Copy Editor: Barbara Feller-Roth
Contributing Proofreaders: Pegi Bevins, Julie Cahalan, Kathy Roth Eastman,
  Terri Krueger
Illustrator: Tom Rosborough
Indexer: Deborah L. Baier
Inputters: Janet Anderson, Connie Webb
Electronic Production Coordinator: Paula Forest
Editorial and Design Assistants: Mary Lee Gavin, Karen McFadden, Kathy Stevens

Meredith® Books
Publisher and Editor in Chief: James D. Blume
Design Director: Matt Strelecki
Managing Editor: Gregory H. Kayko
Executive Editor, Home Improvement and Gardening: Benjamin W. Allen
Executive Editor, Gardening: Michael McKinley

Director, Production: Douglas M. Johnston

Vice President and General Manager: Douglas J. Guendel

Better Homes and Gardens® **Magazine**
Editor in Chief: Karol DeWulf Nickell
Deputy Editor, Gardens and Outdoor Living: Mark Kane

Meredith Publishing Group
President, Publishing Group: Stephen M. Lacy
Vice President-Publishing Director: Bob Mate

Meredith Corporation
Chairman and Chief Executive Officer: William T. Kerr

Chairman of the Executive Committee: E. T. Meredith III

Cover photograph:
John Glover

All of us at Better Homes and Gardens® Books are dedicated to providing you with information and ideas to enhance your home and garden. We welcome your comments and suggestions. Write to us at: Better Homes and Gardens Books, Garden Editorial Department, 1716 Locust St., Des Moines, IA 50309-3023.

If you would like to purchase any of our gardening, cooking, crafts, home improvement, or home decorating and design books, check wherever quality books are sold. Or visit us at bhgbooks.com

introduction

color your world

Color is a matter of perception. The colors you see exist as a result of an eye–brain connection. What truly exists as pure light, human experience tints with meaning. The colors you see have a powerful capacity to paint a rainbow of emotions. This proves especially true in a garden.

No object actually possesses color. A polar bear's fur coat is composed of transparent fibers that reflect light, making them appear white. The ocean is clear water seen as blue because of its depth and how it shines in the sunlight. A rose looks red or yellow to you, but what a bee senses are the radiant markings that will bring it close to the flower's nectar.

Full-color vision probably evolved to help humans identify food and predators, and ultimately to survive. Now it has become the tool for much more leisurely and enjoyable pursuits, such as gardening.

Sir Isaac Newton first explored how humans perceive color. Refracting sunlight through a simple pinprick on paper, he discovered a band, or spectrum, of colors representing unabsorbed light. Newton invented the color wheel to show arrangements within this spectrum. Leonardo da Vinci later developed color theory as a way to explain the contrasting and complementary kinships among colors that he observed in nature.

vibrant monochrome

above right: **Cannas, zinnias, amaranth, and cosmos stand up and sing in a chorus of red within a pocket garden.**

landscape painting

right: **A palette dominated by pinks, gray-greens, and lavenders and anchored with rounded gray boulders and a gazebo colors this gentle landscape.**

Human ability to understand and enjoy color has evolved through time. Early humans were conscious only of primary colors, seeing the world in bloody reds, heavenly blues, and sunny yellows. Those first colors of human experience still have an instinctive pull, but modern life stimulates people by offering more complex palettes in everything from house paint and appliances to flowers.

Like a prism, your own garden reflects the beauty of the world seen through the light of your experience. The colors you choose will translate that vision.

fiery corner
left: **The warm tones of a climbing rose, a redwood arbor, and yellow foxgloves transform a dark corner into an exciting, flowery destination. Glimmering white chairs and the flair of blue accents add finishing touches.**

garden color | **7**

introduction

the garden canvas

When you break ground for a garden, you'll dab your plant paintbrush into both universal and personal responses to color. That language gives you tools to create moods. Energetic oranges and reds, which urge motion and stimulate appetite, fit well along paths and around dining areas. Serene blues and greens induce tranquillity. In a meditation garden or other seating area, they paint the scene with a sense of peace. Like a baroque concerto, pinks and lavenders soothe with harmonious notes. Purples and deep reds introduce mysterious chords. White, seen in a flattering light, offers refuge and cool refreshment.

The palette of plant choices constantly expands as breeders develop new plant varieties. Although new flower and foliage colors don't keep the fast pace of fashion color trends, certain colors enjoy peaks of popularity. Orange flowers and golden, red, and variegated foliage represent current favorites.

flower fashions

above: **This window box wears the hottest trends in annual flowers, including 'Peaches 'n' Cream' verbena, diascia, million bells (Calibrachoa spp.), orange abutilon, and zonal geranium.**

color whimsy

above: Color blooms among the furnishings
of this outdoor dining room. Cheerful
hues of yellow, blue, and green combine
in a cozy setting brimming with smaller,
decorative elements.

pastel fantasy

left: Tranquil color choices of blue and white
create a restful nook inside a front gate.
The white arbor, wrought-iron furnishings,
and salvaged door add dreamlike, timeless
elements. The fountain and drifts of white
flowers make this garden a twilight destination.

introduction

play of light

The landscape's colors may appear dazzling, subdued, or nearly invisible by turns, reacting to the sun's intensity. Every corner of your garden canvas shines when you learn how to play with light: which colors appear radiant at twilight, which look brightest at high noon, and which shine like candles in shade. A true "color gardener" knows how to juggle colors in balance with given light conditions and other natural surroundings.

Terms such as saturation, shade, tone, and tint explain why colors appear bright, dark, similar, or light. As you become familiar with seasonal changes and how the sun moves across your landscape, you'll gain visual skill at staging different colors in the light, deciding when a saturated versus a tinted color, or a pastel versus a bright, best fits in your garden's constantly changing choreography of color and light.

blue moods

right: The skillful use of color extends into every level and aspect of this blue-theme garden, from the latticed arbor to the fence to the knob-head alliums and blue-gray agaves in lead urns.

summer harmonies

below: A border of bright perennials, including Asiatic lilies, lythrum, and monkshood, synchronize their blooming rhythm to the summer sun.

how to use this book

How can you work with your chosen colors, blend them with a contrasting or transitional hue, and segue those brushstrokes into a garden masterpiece? Study the relationships among colors. Gather leaves and flowers from your favorite plants and play with them in a vase or on a sheet of plain paper, juxtaposing textures and hues until you find a balance that pleases your eye. Some garden designers also recommend collecting paint chips in your intended palette and using them to color-match at the garden center as you search out furniture and ornaments.

Use this book to lay the groundwork for your garden. First, explore the qualities and effects of each color and learn which blooms and leaves contain them. Find out which colors work best together, which linking colors to use, and how to contrast or subdue plant colors. Build color relationships that flow throughout the garden.

Discover which plants deliver the most enduring color in the garden. You'll also learn how to sustain colorful plantings throughout the growing season and year-round, as well as how to multiply them to get the most from your color budget. Spend the bulk on trees and shrubs that will provide colorful highlights in more than one season. Get lots of filler color inexpensively by growing annuals from seed.

Travel through the pages to the gardens of five artists who share tips on working with color. Following their footsteps, consider furnishings and accessories to complete your own garden's colorful statement. Then try a project or two and give it your own unique spin. Now take up your garden paintbrush and begin. Your adventures with color start here!

portrait in pinks

left: A vignette of soft pink perennials, such as lythrum, *Lavatera* 'Barnsley', and fragrant phlox, refreshes a midsummer setting.

colors & their companions

pink

*From spring's first trilliums and cherry blossoms to
the last wave of starry asters in a fall border, pink
is a crowd pleaser among flower colors. Always
fresh faced and calming, it links islands of deeper,
more intense colors with soothing tones. Pink serves
as an instant, visual pick-me-up that's reassuring
and cheerful. Many of the garden pinks you know
have softly sentimental echoes: Old Garden roses,
hollyhocks, sweet peas, and foxgloves stand out
among nostalgically favorite pink flowers.*

think pink

- Plant pink flowers around concrete statuary and birdbaths to soften the harsh grayness of the concrete.
- Blossoms of trees and shrubs paint the garden in seasonal spring or summer pink. Redbud, dogwood, weigela, clethra, cherry, crabapple, beautybush, and butterfly bush bear pink blooms.
- Pinks, or dianthus, came by their name not for their rosy coloring but for the flowers' serrated, or pinked, edges.
- Light up the shade with pink-flowering perennials, including astrantia, epimedium, foxglove, bleeding heart, and cyclamen.
- Look no farther than your feet for pink-flowered groundcovers: poppy mallow, creeping thyme, sedum, and heather.

Clockwise, from opposite top:

Rosa × *hybrida*
'Carefree Beauty' rose
This single-petal Griffith Buck rose blooms all summer and endures winter extremes as cold as Zone 4. It traces its heritage to antique pink garden roses.

Rhododendron spp., *Clematis* spp.
'Antoon van Welie' rhododendron, 'Nelly Moser' clematis
Hardy evergreen rhododendrons and azaleas contribute vibrant pinks in spring. The clematis hybrid blooms in late spring and often again in late summer.

Aster novae-angliae
New England aster
A native North American wildflower improved through breeding, this plant is a stalwart of late summer and fall.

Paeonia spp.
peony
Winter chilling prompts this hardy perennial's brief but fragrant spring flowers. Plant the growing points, or eyes, no more than 2 inches deep to ensure blooms.

Digitalis purpurea, *Rosa* spp.
foxglove, unidentified rose
Their light-dark contrasts of pinks make these plants a picture-perfect duo.

pink

The many faces of pink range from the barely-there blush that tints spring crabapple blossoms to the throbbing magenta found in dianthus, portulaca, and hibiscus. If a delicate pink flower in your border deserves more attention, plant it next to white. White spotlights even the palest hues.

Look also on the lighter side of the pink spectrum for effective linking colors. Puddles of light pink enrich adjacent deep blues, golden yellows, and deep cerise pink. The one richly saturated color that doesn't benefit from pink is red. A side-by-side contrast of the two colors ends up looking flat. But if the pink has a peachy cast with tints of yellow, then adjacent red flowers will pop visually.

Use silver foliage as a partner for pink to separate more intense hues in a long flower border. One of pink's most effective harmonies occurs with blues of all shades. Pale hues of pink and blue merge in mauve. Find it in varieties of monkshood, delphinium, hellebore, and lilac. Mauve looks muddy unless woven skillfully into the garden. Deep, saturated pinks, violets, and dark blue help clarify and define mauve; silver sidekicks set off its satiny sheen.

Pink invariably hits it off visually with green. A green, white, and pink planting trio provides instant refreshment. Looking for a good match for hot pink? Try equally jazzy versions of green: lime green or yellow-green. Think magenta zinnias paired with bells of Ireland.

Clockwise, from opposite top:
Astilbe spp.,
Dianthus barbatus
astilbe, sweet William
The 15-inch-tall border pink, or sweet William, comes in vivid shades of magenta and carmine, a beautiful foil to feathery, peachy pink astilbe.

Rosa spp.
'Bonica' Shrub rose
A frothy, pale pink and white border of Shrub roses and perennials romances a split-rail fence at the height of summer.

Rosa spp., *Iris spuria*
'Belinda's Dream' rose, spuria iris
These tall, hardy irises spread in hospitable climates. Their slender yellow blooms synchronize with the first flowering of the Shrub rose in early summer.

Paeonia, Phlox divaricata
peony, woodland phlox
Both of these fragrant perennials flower in late spring or early summer. Plant them in light shade as a bulb cover.

Lilium hybrid
Asiatic lilies
A pink and yellow lily duet freshens up the border in midsummer along with shiny pink lavatera. Plant lilies in fall or early spring.

red

Red tantalizes our impulsive side. It excites and energizes, stirring us with the primal color of fire, sunsets, and blood. Red varies from vermilion and scarlet to crimson and maroon. Its association with passion and prosperity across the globe also gives red cultural significance. Like a flamenco dancer strutting across the stage, red commands attention. Unpredictable and volatile, red inspires risk taking. Need a visual bull's-eye in the border? Opt for red flowers or foliage as the exclamation marks in your garden palette.

Papaver somniferum
breadseed poppy
Scatter annual poppy seed in lawns, meadows, and
flower borders wherever a splash of summer red will
stand out.

Dianthus deltoides
maiden pink
This fragrant member of the carnation family features
bunches of serrated flowers that attract butterflies.
It's a short-lived perennial that's hardy to Zone 3.

Crocosmia masoniorum
'Lucifer' crocosmia
Crocosmia's wands of fiery flowers sprout from bulbs.
Plant after the danger of frost passes; lift and store
indoors before the ground freezes in cold climates.

Zinnia elegans, Canna × hybrida
zinnia, canna
When pairing these two tender plants, use taller zinnia
varieties on the same eye level as the canna flowers. Lift
canna tubers and store them inside in cold-winter areas.

seeing red

- Jarring on a large scale, red tends to dominate
  a scene. Use it sparingly for best results.
- In thin, weak spring light, red brightens the
  entire garden. Summer morning and evening
  light kindles a glow in red petals that appears
  harsh in midday sun. In fall, red looks deeper
  and richer; it has a warming effect.
- Red flowers (especially tubular–shape ones)
  signal hummingbirds that nectar awaits.
- Botanical (Latin) plant names often allude to
  their color. *Cardinalis, coccineus, rosea, rubra, ruber,*
  and *sanguineus* all refer to kinds of red.
- Weave red accents, such as linens and
  candles, into your outdoor living areas for a
  cheery how-do-you-do when company calls.

red

Red takes on different properties depending on what colors you pair with it. The most effective framing color for a red-flowered standout is its complement: green. When a border focuses on green foliage, a single red-flower or red-leaf accent truly shines.

Include red in your garden's color scheme by partnering it with silver or white. Silver calms red into good behavior in a border; white offers a crisp contrast to richly colored reds

Write mystery into your garden plots by combining the deep reds, such as burgundy, maroon, and russet, with equally dark purple and chocolate brown. Such sultry combinations create the illusion of depth and hidden distances.

Red berries, twigs, and bark create magic in the winter garden against a snowy background.

Clockwise, from opposite top:

Tulipa spp., *Muscari* spp.
tulip, grape hyacinth
A red and blue medley delivers strong color to early-spring gardens. Plant masses of these hardy bulbs in late fall.

Lobelia spp.,
Perovskia **hybrid**
lobelia, Russian sage
Featuring the same spiky silhouette, these two perennials pair in a striking combo.

Sedum 'Autumn Joy',
Aster × frikartii 'Monch',
stonecrop,
Frikart's aster
Lavender and red-orange warm the fall garden with perennial color. The asters' golden centers echo the fuzzy texture of the sedum blooms.

Knautia macedonica,
Anethum graveolens
pincushion, dill
The burgundy perennial and the yellow annual feature similar wiry stems.

Salvia farinacea,
S. splendens
mealycup sage,
scarlet sage
Many of summer's richest hues come from the blue and red blooms of annual salvias.

orange

Orange mixes the cheerfulness of yellow and the boldness of red into an attention-grabbing burst of volcanic energy. Hot orange's tropical nature and its universal popularity, especially in Latin cultures, has made it a sought-after garden and fashion color. Orange appeals for its sunlit radiance and for the way it piques our appetite. The color, which includes pumpkins, peaches, and citrus in its culinary repertoire, also attracts hummingbirds and butterflies when it appears in flowers.

let orange shine

- Orange holds its own in sunny, bright exposures. Choose hot orange flowers for hot climates and softer peaches and apricots for regions that frequently experience cool, cloudy weather.

- Because orange enhances appetite and promotes sociability, plant plenty of orange-flowering plants near outdoor eating areas.

- Incorporate orange into your garden by using brick walls and paths, terra-cotta pots and statuary, and copper trellises and birdbaths.

- Include plants that bear orange fruits: pyracantha, sea buckthorn, and bittersweet, as well as some roses and hollies.

Clockwise, from opposite top:

Papaver nudicaule
Iceland poppy

A perennial, often biennial, this cold-climate poppy unfurls rich-hue, silken flowers atop 2- to 3-foot-tall stems during late spring's cool weather.

Cosmos sulphureus
'Klondike' cosmos

Easily grown from seed, this dwarf annual offers waves of brilliant orange throughout the summer.

Lilium hybrid
Asiatic lily

This intense orange bloomer harmonizes with white, pink, pale orange, or blue summer flowers.

Asclepias tuberosa
butterfly weed (milkweed)

Flower clusters on these lanky plants open in mid- to late summer and attract droves of butterflies.

Kniphofia
red hot poker

Brush-shape, tubular flowers characterize this heat-hardy perennial. The varied combinations of red, orange, and yellow flowers attract hummingbirds.

orange

Bring out the best in both bold and pale oranges by blending them with their color wheel complement: blue. When you contrast fiery orange flowers with blue and yellow ones, the border sizzles. Deep blue *Salvia farinacea* combined with orange-yellow calendula or peachy verbascum results in a magnificent effect. You'll get comparably classic results from a trio of orange, red, and blue.

Purple also marries with orange in a sophisticated color composition. Both contain red values, ensuring compatibility. Sometimes the colors crop up on the same plant, as in the magnificent multitints of *Euphorbia griffithii* 'Fireglow'. On the blue side of purple, lilacs and lavenders also flatter deep orange.

Mingle orange flowers with pink and you end up with a plant painting that's

slightly dissonant but delicious. Add white or pale yellow to knit the two other colors together. Similarly, cream and bronze partners moderate orange. Orange and white duos create vignettes with a fresh feel. If the white flowers have orange or yellow centers, the match works even better.

Combining orange with lime green brings out the yellow values in both colors. This duet works wonderfully in the shade when the orange blooms of trollius, azalea, or tiger lily stand out among chartreuse foliage. Complete this sensational shady scenario by adding purple-leaf plants.

Pale orange hues, such as peach, salmon, and apricot, harmonize happily with silver-leaf plants, especially in cloudy climates. Imagine peach-color roses skirted with artemisia, rue, or lavender. 'Southern Charms' verbascum or 'Brompton Apricot' stock combine peach-color petals and silvery foliage all in one.

Clockwise, from opposite top:
Lilium hybrid,
Silene spp.
Asiatic lily, catchfly
This early-summer scenario entails planting drifts of lilac around the feet of lilies. An annual native to America, silene self-seeds freely.

Cosmos sulphureus,
Salvia guaranitica
cosmos, salvia
This complementary pair thrives in the summer heat. The salvia survives mild winters only; otherwise, it's best grown as an annual.

Eschscholzia spp.,
Leucanthemum ×
superbum
California poppy,
Shasta daisy
Sow poppy seeds on hillsides, in vacant lots, or in country gardens and celebrate summer as their gleaming petals unfurl. Shasta daisy spreads in undisturbed areas too.

Abutilon hybrid,
Ageratum houstonianum
flowering maple, 'Blue Horizon' flossflower
The tall, billowy blossom annual grows to just the right height to mingle with abutilon, a tender tropical that can move indoors over winter.

Calendula officinalis,
Antirrhinum hybrid
pot marigold,
snapdragon
Enjoy the flower power as these annuals keep up their show throughout summer and fall.

yellow

Yellow delivers an invitation to smile. It never fails to cheer. As the color closest to that of the sun, it's only fitting that yellow announces the spring with a deluge of daffodils and forsythias, and then rules over the summer garden with unflagging brightness. It closes the fall as the last golden leaf twirls to the ground. Yellow emanates a sense of well-being that's instantly, and joyously, absorbed. If smiles and hopes had a color, it would be called yellow.

Clockwise, from opposite top:
Helianthus annuus
annual sunflower

Sunflowers epitomize the summer season. Include 3-foot-tall dwarf varieties, such as 'Teddy Bear' and 'Sunspot', in your summer yellow paintbox for excellent cut flowers.

Lysimachia punctata
yellow loosestrife (circleflower)

This heirloom, prized by pioneer Americans, thrives in partial sun and moist soil. The 3-foot-tall golden-flowering perennial can become invasive.

Thunbergia alata
black-eyed Susan vine

Grown from seed, this tropical annual drapes a hanging basket, window box, or trellis for the summer. It fares best in a sunny spot with regular watering.

Hemerocallis hybrid, *Heliopsis helianthoides*
'Hyperion' daylily, 'Golden Feathers'
false sunflower

This monochromatic planting of bright and pale yellows pairs perennials timed to bloom in early summer. Gain more plants by digging and splitting mature plants every third spring.

Acer palmatum
Japanese maple

These colorful, slow-growing small trees thrive in moist soil and shade. Plant them under oaks with azaleas and ferns for a woodland effect.

harness the power of yellow

- Yellow increases a sense of space. A narrow side yard or dim courtyard takes on a bright new look when it features plantings with a yellow theme.
- Yellow appears fresh and radiant on the hottest days. Use yellow flowers and leaves in window boxes and baskets to create a warm, cheerful look.
- Pale yellows illuminate night gardens. Welcome the moonshine potential of such flowers as 'Moonbeam' coreopsis, evening primrose, *Brugmansia*, santolina, 'Anthea' or 'Moonshine' yarrow, and 'Lady Banks' rose.
- Fill in with green-and-yellow variegated foliage to showcase neighboring flowers of purple, bright pink, or red.

garden color | 27

yellow

Although we normally think of yellow
as an intense color that can overpower,
use paler shades to link other, brighter
colors effectively. Pale creamy yellow
has a calming influence on other flower
colors. Combine it with pale pink, blue,
or white, especially in cool, overcast
climates where more gaudy shades of
yellow appear jarring. An all-yellow
planting combining different shades looks
cheerful yet sophisticated.

Yellow radiates in the shade where it
pairs beautifully with pale greens, lime
green, or green-yellow or green-white
variegated foliage. Strong yellows for
shady places include Japanese maple,
kerria, ligularia, lysimachia, azalea, and
rhododendron.

Increased plant choices in yellow-
foliage varieties also now exist. The glow
of golden-leaf shrubs, such as barberry
or euonymous, among the greens turns
up the wattage in a foliage garden. Here,

yellow leaves provide the visual interest that flowers usually supply.

When bright yellow joins up with orange and its complement, blue, it sets an energetic harmony into motion. Yellow enhances both colors. When it contains a hint of orange, yellow becomes a showstopping dance partner with bright or light blue. The blue slightly mutes yellow's boldness and brings out its luminescence.

The same effect happens with yellow's opposites on the color wheel: purple and dark red. They look even better when seen in the company of yellow. Generously sprinkle yellows, both pale and bright, in areas exposed to early- or late-day sunlight, when yellow reflects rather than absorbs light.

Clockwise, from opposite top:
Hydrangea macrophylla, Rudbeckia hirta, Lilium hybrid
bigleaf hydrangea (mophead), black-eyed Susan, Asiatic lily
This trio brightens a cloudy-climate garden. Plant the medley of shrub, perennial, and bulb in spring and enjoy the way it warms the gray concrete accent for summers to come.

Allium spp., *Lilium* hybrid
flowering onion, Asiatic lily
Flowering bulbs in complementary colors make a sensational duo for early-summer gardens. The lily acts as a natural stake for the slender allium stalk.

Solidago spp., *Echinacea* spp.
goldenrod, purple coneflower
Partnered with another native prairie perennial, goldenrod fills the border with flowers that echo the color of late-summer sunshine.

Rosa hybrid, *Myosotis scorpioides*
'Graham Thomas' rose, forget-me-not
Delicate sprays of perennial forget-me-nots fill in the gaps among English roses. Bright blue and apricot flowers invariably make a stunning combination.

green

Green frames the jewel-like beauty of flowers so well that you might take its shady reassurance and new-leaf innocence for granted. Most garden color flows from nature's cornucopia of greens, from mosses and groundcovers to leafy shrubs and trees. Sophisticated garden designs often rely on green's infinite variety. Sunlight plays out a daily drama, transmuting vital greens to liquid golds or forest-dark, deep mysteries by turns.

Clockwise, from opposite top:

Lysimachia congestiflora
variegated creeping Jenny
A collage of variegated gold-and-green lysimachia, along with chartreuse hosta leaves and two varieties of fern, provides a perennial tapestry in the shade.

Iris sibirica, Matteuccia struthiopteris
Siberian iris, ostrich fern
Two perennials for rich, moist soil unfurl their new green finery and flowers in late spring.

Petroselinum spp.
parsley
As the first color of spring in the kitchen garden, a contrast of flat- and curly-leaf biennial parsley creates a textural study in green. Mulching plants lightly in fall helps them survive winter.

Hebe cupressoides, Juniperus spp.
hebe, juniper
Rugged evergreen groundcovers, including hebes and junipers, join creeping thymes to show off various tints of green combined with flattering hues of bronze and gold.

Acer palmatum
Japanese maple
An excellent understory tree, the Japanese maple's leaves unfold like graceful fans.

the planting o' the green

- Choose green arbors, benches, fencing, furniture, and containers whenever possible. They'll enhance nearby flower colors.
- Contrast different shades of green foliage in deep shade, where some of the showiest flowering plants won't thrive. Use chartreuse, yellow, and variegated green–white or yellow–green foliage plants for the most pronounced effects. Add light-color statuary, a birdbath, a bench, or a temporary pot of vibrant flowers to make this area of your garden shine.
- Green flowers offer novel appeal. Try viburnum, lady's mantle, tulip, hellebore, bells of Ireland, and hydrangea. These make great cut flowers too.
- Many plants lend their names to shades of green, including pea, olive, fern, bean, lime, kiwi, mint, and ivy. It's no wonder there's a green named spring!

garden color | **31**

green

The green season begins with the pale green cones
of uncurling hostas and coils of fiddlehead ferns.
Summer deepens new green into mature shades.
Boulders, tree trunks, and ponds may disclose the
startling lime green of lichens, mosses, and algae.
Mediterranean and other dry-climate plants offer a
palette of dusty gray-greens that diffuse the sun's
burning rays through summer's hottest days.

Green makes shady places appear fresh and
cool, especially when the picture is woven with
white flowers or variegated foliage. Two-tone
leaves that pair green with white, silver, or gold
dapple the shade with bright highlights. In coleus,
houttuynia, and tovara leaves, green mingles with
reds, purples, and blues, resulting in a wide palette
of possibilities for shade.

Consider nearby greens when placing intense
flower colors in the border. Green tinged with red
ensures an effective union between deep, dramatic
red and purple or yellow and purple. Chartreuse
or yellow-green foliage brings out the best in
purple and yellow combos. The blue-green of hosta
and yucca leaves flatters pastels and (in generous
portions) makes small spaces appear larger.

Clockwise, from opposite top:

Sedum spurium
creeping sedum
Fine-textured perennial creeping sedum
thrives in a cracked concrete birdbath that
no longer holds water.

Juniperus horizontalis 'Wiltonii'
horizontal blue juniper
Among a colorful cast of shrub characters,
including Harry Lauder's walking stick,
blue spruce, chartreuse false cypress, and
'Mugo' pine, groundcover juniper sprawls at
center stage.

Hydrangea spp., *Hosta* hybrid
hydrangea, hosta
Layers and shades of green dotted with white
and orange glow in this shady oasis that also
includes lilies, impatiens, and coral bells.

Pelargonium spp., *Impatiens* hybrid
'Peppermint Star' geranium, impatiens
The textures of two annuals form a dynamic
contrast. Chartreuse geranium foliage frames
and clarifies red impatiens blossoms.

Pinus spp., *Acaena* spp., *Imperata cylindrica*
pine, bidi–bidi, Japanese blood grass
Not a flower in sight, yet this interplay of
textures from an ornamental grass, a perennial
groundcover, and an evergreen renders an
always fresh and intriguing composition.

blue

Blue offers peaceful depths for our contemplation.

Heavenly blue has a spiritual side that evokes serenity and inspires wonder. Promising limitless horizons in water, sky, and garden borders, it invites the beholder to wade in and get lost. Cool, calming blue anchors hotter, more emotional colors in pools of natural tranquillity. Blue fascinates as it dances with light. Spring's pale light brings out the silvery side of blue. In the heat of summer, blue appears clear and bright—refreshing as a mountain lake.

get the garden blues

- Clear blues emerge in spring forget-me-nots and columbines; campanulas give way to irises in early summer. As high summer approaches, bold blues take over with aconite, baptisia, clematis, and delphinium.
- Add blue to your landscape in the form of ornamental fruits: blueberry, porcelain berry, bayberry, and juniper.
- In hot, dry climates, blue appears as strong and limitless as the sky. In damp regions, blue and green merge. In shade and at dusk, blues seem violet, whereas violet seems pink, so place cool-color plants in areas where they'll shine true.

Clockwise, from opposite top:

Muscari spp.
grape hyacinth
Plant the tiny bulbs in fall and enjoy the exceptional spring display of blooms. Place masses of bulbs under fruit trees, along edges of beds, or in a rock garden.

Salvia uliginosa
bog sage
This brilliant blue-flower perennial thrives in damp soil with a sunny exposure. Grow it as an annual for fall color in cold-climate areas.

Convolvulus spp.
morning glory
The intensely sky blue flower saucers on this annual vine have made it an all-time favorite for generations of gardeners.

Delphinium elatum
delphinium hybrids
Delphiniums require a bit of pampering to produce their regal, perennial flower spikes. Stake each plant to support the flowers throughout their summer show.

Hydrangea macrophylla
mophead hydrangea
Unsurpassable for summer color in the shade, hydrangea shrubs produce flower clusters in shades of pink, blue, or white, depending on the variety and the soil pH.

garden color | **35**

blue

Blue's recessive quality serves as a beautiful blender for other colors and makes it appear warm or cool relative to its tint and plant companions. Cool, pale blue flowers, especially those that appear in spring, knit other colors together. For subtle, impressionistic contrasts, combine blue with its cool cousins: lavender, gray, and green.

Blue, in any hue, mingles well with pink, yellow, and its opposite: orange. Borders painted with blue, yellow, and orange or a trio of blue, red, and lime green, add pizzazz to summer landscapes. Blue has a stabilizing effect when placed near electric colors such as chartreuse, magenta, crimson, or hot pink.

The frosty blues of fall that tint ornamental kale and Russian sage interact dramatically with other autumnal colors, including deep oranges, reds, and violets.

As intermediary colors in the garden, blue and silver work well together, creating restful scenes where eyes can take refuge. The two colors merge in the foliage of plants such as rue, juniper, blue fescue, *Rosa glauca*, and *Hosta sieboldiana*. Blue–flower plants with silvery foliage, including lupine, baptisia, pulmonaria, mertensia, and many salvias, have a double impact on the landscape. Like silver, white clarifies blue's ambiguity. Blue and white combinations bond easily, creating a crisp, polished look.

It's that visual ambiguity that makes blue the perfect vehicle for conjuring illusions of depth. Placed at a border's end, or in the background, it creates an impression that the space goes on and on. If you want to connect your garden's boundaries and the surrounding landscape, blue provides a gentle blending tool. Establish a contemplative area around a fountain or garden bench by using tranquil blue flowers and foliage.

Clockwise, from opposite top:
Nepeta spp., *Salvia* spp., *Artemisia* spp.
catmint, salvia, artemisia
A restful planting focuses on this flower-bearing statue, surrounding it with a sea of blue and gray textures from hardy perennials.

Antirrhinum hybrid, *Salvia farinacea*
snapdragon, mealycup sage
These annuals work well as a combo because of their similar flower shape and the inherent synergy of blue and yellow.

Platycodon grandiflorus,
Achillea spp.,
balloon flower, yarrow
Perennial blue balloon flower and golden yarrow combine with orange lilies in a summer meadow that sizzles with color.

Cistus × *purpureus*, *Ceanothus* spp.
rock rose, California lilac
The satiny pink flowers of rock rose and the soft gray-blue of ceanothus announce spring in West Coast gardens. Both shrubs rarely survive below-freezing temperatures.

purple

Majestic purple reigns as the garden peacemaker, marrying colors that often refuse to get along. The purple that streaks twilight's curtains evokes a melancholy stillness. More than any other color, purple gives the impression of texture. Purple is associated with a velvety feel, like the sueded petals of a pansy. Some people think purple too melodramatic and avoid it; others overindulge. But purple has a place in any garden.

playing with purple

- Purple foliage adds a compelling dimension to the garden. Consider purple varieties of ajuga, bergenia, smokebush, barberry, coral bells, snakeroot, geranium, and New Zealand flax.
- Because purple tends to get lost in the shade, pair it with a light-color companion, such as one with chartreuse or golden foliage.
- Smoky purples look their most regal in the fall, especially underplanting Japanese maples and other trees with brilliant red or gold leaves.
- Seek higher-power purples in vines: wisteria, clematis, sweet potato vine, and the dark-leaf grape (*Vitis vinifera* 'Purpurea').

Clockwise, from opposite top:

***Viola* × *wittrockiana* pansy**
This beloved annual perks up spring and fall gardens with its friendly faces. Pansies and other violas are naturally blue, purple, and lavender. Breeders raided the crayon box to give us pansies of every color.

***Heliotropium arborescens* common heliotrope**
Prized for its sweet vanilla-tinged fragrance, heliotrope develops dense flower heads of purple or white in summer. Bring it indoors for the winter.

***Veronica* hybrid 'Sunny Border Blue' speedwell**
Spikes of deep violet-blue stud this glossy-leaf perennial through the summer and into fall.

***Scaevola aemula* fan flower**
With pot-bursting vigor, this Australian native develops cascades of lavender-blue flowers.

***Geranium* hybrid 'Johnson's Blue' cranesbill**
A vital source of early-season blue-violet, this 18-inch-tall perennial blooms through the fall.

purple

Purple spans a wide range, from deep, velvety hues that appear almost black to pale periwinkle. Red-dominated hues of purple add suspense and drama to plantings. They also mediate, bridging the gap between related colors that form dissonant matches on their own, such as red and orange. Blue-violets anchor and visually blend brighter colors.

Purple's ideal partner, yellow, invariably lightens and brightens a scene. Purple and yellow announce spring's arrival in the blooms of bulbs and pansies. Yellow helps to solidify purple, whereas purple subdues yellow. This relationship of contrasts becomes more important in shade-dappled gardens, where purple would easily melt into the shadows without yellow to clarify it. White also stabilizes purple in shade gardens.

Other colors with yellow-dominant tints also flatter and define purple. Similarly, chartreuse plants make good partners. Purple and orange placed together send the color sparks flying in a match that's sultry and sophisticated.

Purple rounds out many effective trios. Plant it with chartreuse and pink for a sense of depth. When blended with blues and greens, it adds substance. Purple anchors combinations of red and gold, making them appear subtle and mysterious. Purple adds weight and value in a flower border. Use it as a shading tool to separate and define other colors.

Purple-leaf plants have become a huge trend in garden design. They offer a varied and versatile palette of trees, shrubs, and ornamental grasses, as well as perennials, annuals, and groundcovers. Incorporate purple-foliage plants into borders and backgrounds just as you would purple flowers to create a powerful sense of drama.

Clockwise, from opposite top:
Monarda didyma
bee balm
Reddish-purple bee balm, backed by a burgundy-leaf ornamental plum tree and edged with ornamental oregano, forms a dramatic summer scene.

Clematis × jackmanii
clematis
Vining clematis includes an array of species and hybrids—many with purple flowers. This large-flowering hybrid is one of the hardiest.

Thymus spp., Alchemilla mollis
thyme, lady's mantle
These hardy, sun-loving perennials meld in waves of purple, yellow, and green.

Campanula spp., Achillea spp.,
peach-leaf and clustered bellflowers, yarrow
Trim perennial bellflowers after their first bloom. You may see second flowerings that keep pace with yarrow's golden blooms.

Muscari spp., Caltha palustris
grape hyacinth, marsh marigold
Among spring's first flowering bulbs, this bold duo makes a splendid show.

lavender

Serene lavender brings a luster to the garden. It holds just enough white to capture and reflect light in a magical way. Beware of lavender's split personality: In the warm light of sunrise or sunset, it seems pink; in the cool light after sunset or in shade, it appears blue. Like the herb that bears its name, lavender stimulates the senses while it calms the mind. It does the work of a garden mediator, making peace among brasher colors. Give lavender a chance to make an impression by combining it with its relatives: violet, lilac, mauve, and purple.

Clockwise, from opposite top:

Clematis **spp.**
'Ramona' clematis
Plant this vining perennial near a tree or shrub and it will entwine itself through the branches. Protect the sensitive clematis crown from diseases and damage by planting it just above the soil line.

Lavandula angustifolia
English lavender
This fragrant herb requires a well-drained soil in a full-sun location. Cut back plants in spring to spur growth.

Allium senescens
flowering onion
The allium grows from a bulb and reaches heights of 3 to 24 inches. Lily stalks make strong living supports for the taller, top-heavy allium stems.

Dianthus **spp.,** *Nepeta* × *faassenii*
'Bath's Pink' dianthus, catmint
This perennial duet blooms in early summer. Both plants have ground-hugging habits and do well in dry soils.

Petunia multiflora
petunia
Fertilize this showy annual often, and cut back leggy plants in midsummer to promote continuous cascades of fragrant flowers.

brush on the lavender

- Plant breeders haven't yet achieved a true blue rose, but lavender varieties come close. Consider pale 'Sterling Silver', 'Angel Face', and 'Lagerfeld'.
- The globe-shape flowers of onion family members, alliums and chives, span the lavender color spectrum. Try as many as you like.
- Lavender, in both name and hue, combines with silver- and gold-foliage plants to form borders that shimmer in the light.
- On the pinkish side of lavender, mauve's tonal ambiguities pose color-blending opportunities in the garden. Designers recommend using splashes of mauve flowers as dividers between deeper colors in a border.

garden color | **43**

lavender

As the most common flower color, lavender has many faces. It cools to a periwinkle blue in the flowers of *Vinca minor* and warms to a reddish mauve in clematis or pansy blossoms. Lavender abounds among the blossoms of herbs, from chives and hyssop to thyme, catmint, and sage.

Lavender forms harmonies with its cousins in the color spectrum: deep violet and magenta. Pale lavender creates soothing pastel scenarios when paired with white, pink, or pale yellow. Bluer shades of lavender shine when warmed by the company of complementary yellow-orange or peach. Planted near silver foliage, lavender looks luminous.

One weakness of lavender: It tends to fade into a dull haze en masse. Prevent this occurrence by interplanting it with bolder colors such as crimson or gold. Yellow makes a perfect partner. (Picture lavender and pale yellow violas that sport both colors in their spring blooms.) Chocolate brown foliage mixed with lavender flowers results in a spectacular marriage. At first blush, pink and lavender might seem too rosy a garden color scheme,

but it's a combination that works. Lavender larkspur glows next to pink coneflower. Add white or sky blue to balance the pink tones. Mauve also goes well with cream, buff, gray, and pink.

Lavender enhances the fall garden's earth tones of bronze, orange, and gold with a touch of the ethereal, represented by perennial asters, fall crocuses, and aconites.

Clockwise, from opposite top:
Aster × frikartii
aster
Asters provide late-season shades of lavender in the garden. This compact variety doesn't need staking.

Rosa **spp.,** *Digitalis* **spp.**
rose, foxglove
Biennial foxglove grows one year and blooms the next.

Iris × germanica
bearded iris (antique variety)
The iris lasts for decades in the garden. Dividing the rhizomes every few years keeps plants vigorous.

Lavandula **spp.,** *Artemisia* **spp.,** *Cynara cardunculus*
lavender, artemisia, cardoon
Mediterranean natives such as these perennials fare best in rocky soil and a sunny location.

Echinacea **spp.,** *Consolida ambigua*
purple coneflower, larkspur
Sow annual larkspur seeds once; the plants will self-sow and return on their own in subsequent years.

white

White blends the intensity of all colors into light itself. Although white is not a color per se, it embodies simplicity and symbolizes purity. Crisp and refreshing on a summer afternoon, white also has a mysterious side that comes out to play by the light of the moon. As the evening deepens, white lights up. Many white-flowering plants have a fragrant bonus: Their intoxicating perfumes lure people as well as flying pollinators into the night garden.

Clockwise, from
opposite top:
*Datura meteloides,
Nicotiana sylvestris*
**datura, flowering
tobacco**
These tender plants
exude exotic perfumes.
But beware of datura
leaves and sap—
they're poisonous.

Anemone japonica
Japanese anemone
A tall white highlight in
fall gardens, this perennial
also flowers in pink and
mauve. It spreads quickly
in moist, enriched soils
and does especially well
in semishaded areas.

Ammi majus
Queen Anne's lace
This annual fills meadow
gardens with swaying
stalks of lace in mid- to
late summer. A relative
of the carrot, it has a
taproot and doesn't
transplant well, but it
reseeds gregariously.

Rosa hybrid
'Iceberg' rose
Dependable for landscape
uses such as hedging, this
Floribunda rose produces
multiflower branches of
delicate white all summer.

Nicotiana alata
jasmine tobacco
The frilled flower tubes
on this tall, hardy tobacco
fill the evening air with a
sweet, tropical perfume.
It thrives in partial shade.

ways to use white

- Highlight a focal point at the end of a path
  with white flowers or a white container.
- Among the most spectacular white-flower
  trees for landscapes: davidia, snowbell,
  magnolia, and dogwood. Some birches
  feature white trunks.
- Against the backdrop of a white fence,
  paint with the boldest plant colors
  possible, such as orange and scarlet.
- Light up your garden with white versions
  of these common plants: ageratum, cosmos,
  heliotrope, rhododendron, clematis, bee
  balm, and bleeding heart.
- Embroider white lace into your borders
  with these airy white flowers: rockcress,
  baby's breath, 'The Pearl' yarrow, and
  gooseneck loosestrife.

white

White brings out the true hues of any color with which it's paired. On the other hand, place a white flower next to green and it takes on a greenish tinge. The same phenomenon happens with yellow, pink, or blue. White has many personalities; it takes colorful companions to bring out white's myriad possibilities. Yellow-tinted white, or cream, harmonizes with almost every other flower color, as does variegated cream-and-green foliage.

An all-white garden cools and calms. Some gardeners design elegant white-flower refuges. A simple white palette paints borders with endless intrigue when white flowers mingle with a variety of leaf textures and colors: the bold with the fine (white coneflowers with lacy white yarrow), the

diminutive with the smooth (candytuft with hostas). Large white flowers, such as lilies or matilija poppy, lift the garden's horizon with simple, bold focal points. The delicate finery of baby's breath, Queen Anne's lace, or snow-in-summer breaks up reflected light for an effect of glimmering romance.

A popular choice for garden furniture and structures, clean, bright white says: "Welcome. Sit here. Walk this way."

Silver and silvery blue set off white, illuminating it. Although white provides a luminous divider for other colors, it can appear dimmed in gray climates. Avoid an overabundance of white in desert climates by subduing its harsh glare with equal amounts of silver and green.

Clockwise, from opposite top:
Convallaria majalis
lily-of-the-valley
A perennial groundcover bearing stalks of fragrant white bells. Dividing the plants every few years keeps them vigorous and productive. It thrives in shade.

Lavatera trimestris, Chrysanthemum parthenium
'Mont Blanc' mallow, matricaria
Annual mallow, a relative of the hollyhock, grows to 20 inches tall and produces abundant flowers, good for cutting. Matricaria prefers some shade and regular watering.

Rosa moschata, Allium multibulbosum
'Penelope' Musk rose, flowering onion
June brings the first blooms of this fragrant rose, timed with flower spheres of the tall allium. Hardy to Zone 5, 'Penelope' continues to bloom through the fall.

Leucanthemum × *superbum, Lysimachia punctata*
Shasta daisy, yellow loosestrife
Shasta daisies lighten up borders. The perennial loosestrife becomes a nuisance in damp soil.

garden color | **49**

silver

Silver adds a sprinkle of stardust to the most earthbound garden scenes. Spun from gray's whiter, less somber side, silver lightens and unifies. It binds plantings together in a dynamic play of light. Drifts of silver also act like storm clouds in the border, casting mysterious and ambiguous reflections, especially as the daylight dims. Silver-leaf plants, native to hot and sunny climes, look leaden in rainy areas; placed in a sunny spot, however, silver weaves endless enchantments.

strike a soft note with silver

- Grow these silver-leaf plants for their form: cardoon, clary sage, and globe thistle.
- Many silver-leaf plants, especially those with aromatic foliage, don't attract hungry deer. The deer-repelling list includes salvia, lavender, rosemary, and yarrow.
- Include plenty of silver spillers and cascading edgers, such as 'Silver Brocade' artemisia, snow-in-summer, silver thyme, lamb's-ears, germander, and lamium, in your borders and containers.
- Gray or silver embellishments, such as concrete statuary, mirrorlike water, or galvanized metal, act as ideal foils for plants.

Clockwise, from opposite top:
Artemisia **hybrid**
'Powis Castle' artemisia
Forming low mounds of ethereal silver lace, this perennial edges beds while highlighting and contrasting with masses of bright colors.

Senecio cineraria
dusty miller
The silver-sueded leaves of this annual weave texture into beds and containers. Remove flower stalks from this mounding plant to keep foliage vigorous.

Helichrysum petiolare
licorice plant
Winter hardy only in the warmest climates of Southern California and Florida, this fuzzy-leaf vining annual works well in potted schemes. Try chartreuse 'Limelight' or gold-and-green variegated forms.

Artemisia ludoviciana albula
'Silver King' artemisia
This tall, shrubby plant produces branches of aromatic foliage and enhances perennial borders with silvery, light-catching effects. Use it in dried arrangements and for wreath bases.

silver

Silver enchants green-dominated landscapes, visually underlining variations in greens that would otherwise go unnoticed. In hot, arid regions, silver stands in for green as the staple foliage color. Fuzzy silver-leaf plants have hairs that insulate against summer's heat and drought. This hairy coating gives silver its special reflective qualities.

Silver plants, whether the jagged leaves of an artichoke and its relatives, thistle and cardoon, or the wispy lace of 'Powis Castle' artemisia, weave fascinating textures into the border. Who can resist touching the plush leaves of lamb's-ears, a favorite silver edger?

Almost any color scheme has space for silver, but it blends especially well with pastels: pale pinks, blues, yellows, lavender, and white. Silver's ethereal appearance makes pastels stand out like lighted candles.

As a foil to brilliant-color flowers, silver cools and tames. It brings together hot hues that otherwise appear garish. Silver-splattered foliage plants, including pulmonaria and lamium, also put a shine in the border. They're even more valuable because of their tolerance for shade.

Clockwise, from opposite top:

Artemisia spp., *Echinacea purpurea*, *Eryngium* spp.
artemisia, 'White Swan' coneflower, sea holly
These hardy perennials thrive in the summer's worst heat. Harvest the artemisia foliage and sea holly flower heads for dried arrangements.

Geranium hybrid, *Pulmonaria saccharata*
'Johnson's Blue' cranesbill, 'Spilled Milk' lungwort
Both perennials form compact mounds, growing low to the ground. The lungwort flowers in early spring, but its foliage stays showy all summer.

Stachys byzantina
lamb's-ears
In a sunny location and adequately drained soil, it spreads vigorously. To keep the leaves large and showy, remove flower spikes when they form.

Artemisia spp., *Achillea* spp.
artemisia, yarrow
Both of these perennials have aromatic foliage and repel deer. They flourish in sunny, dry conditions. Remove faded flowers from yarrow to induce new blooms.

Pelargonium hybrid, *Helichrysum petiolare*
common geranium, 'White Licorice' helichrysum
Soft-leaf helichrysum grows assertively and dominates a container planting. Enjoy these annuals as long as they last.

rainbow

Vibrant, joyous colors flow throughout the garden and the seasons. The brilliant display starts with a burst of multicolor flowering bulbs in spring. By midsummer, it reaches a glorious crescendo. Bold and brilliant clusters of yellow, blue, red, purple, magenta, and more make harmonies and contrasts. Dense layers of color result in a horticultural masterpiece. Despite surprise combinations, there is a sense of balance in the patchwork garden. The overall effect is persistently cheerful.

colorful crowd

opposite: Almost every color earns the spotlight in this Canadian garden anchored by hardy roses, 'Morden Centennial' and 'Winnipeg Parks'. Drifts of allium, lemony 'Connecticut King' and pink 'Malta' Asiatic lilies fill in bare spots with midsummer color.

all-season rainbows

left: A skillful mix of perennials and annuals in layers achieves full and colorful effects. Perennials, such as the delphiniums and lilies, build the garden's form and architecture, whereas the annuals (dianthus, pansy, and geranium) expand it outward with bold splashes of summer color. The purple-flower edging of campanula and lobelia ties all the hues together.

growing rainbows

- Grow spectacular rainbow gardens by starting with garden gold: fertile soil, well amended with compost, rotted manure, and chopped leaves. Build raised beds with quality topsoil where the native soil is extremely poor (sandy, clayey, or otherwise poorly draining).

- Manage your horticultural masterpiece by planting dense layers of color. Group long-blooming plants according to their heights, as in a class photo: short in front, tall in back, others in between.

- Liberal plantings of green and white, working as neutral backgrounds or blenders, help make a multicolor scheme successful.

- Allow a couple of colors, such as blue and purple or pink, to dominate. Repeat plants and combinations in a border garden, to achieve dense splashes of color in patterns.

rainbow

Although they look casually composed, rainbow–color gardens disguise some careful sleight of hand. There's a knack to stringing colors, heights, and textures together into a unified design. Start with solid anchors in the form of roses and other shrubs that bring constant color into the border either via flowers or foliage or both. Then introduce perennials for form and color compatibility with the shrubs. Complete the garden's design with colorful outbursts of annuals.

Think of your color scheme as a patchwork quilt that comes together block by block. Design each block with annuals that echo or contrast with perennial flowers and foliage colors. Stitch each block to the next with threads of pink, white, silver, lavender, or green, those valuable linking colors.

Many garden designers use the technique of drift planting. This strategy takes triangular groupings of three, five, or seven plants of a single type, and preferably one color, and interweaves them with other triangles. For a more natural look,

plant list

1 foxglove

2 lychnis

3 red hot poker

4 petunia

5 geranium

6 daisy

7 false sunflower

8 iris

stretch out the far corner of the triangle so that the last plant grows into the adjacent grouping. Drifts fit best in large, open beds rather than narrow borders.

Finish the border's edges with unifying colors from flowers and from foliage plants. Foliage also comes in handy for filling bare spots next to roses or between young perennial plants.

If you need help planning your next garden, you can find the perfect combination of colors and plants in garden plans at **www.bhg.com/ bkgardenplans**

painting with plants
left and *opposite:* This garden illustrates a painterly technique: Blocks of color fit into an overall plan by harmonizing or contrasting with adjacent plants. Irises, red hot pokers, and red geraniums pour on the hot color, contrasting with cool-blossom petunias, foxgloves, daisies, and irises.

garden color | **57**

schemes
& themes

bold

unrestrained passion

Bold plant couples engage in the horticultural equivalent of passionate love affairs. Shocking! The usual rules fly out the window. Introduce one intense color to another and you have instant fireworks in the garden. The bold garden creates a sense of ongoing drama. It's a place where the most unexpected matches merge in sizzling synchronicity. Restrained gardeners who prefer neat-edge borders and pale palettes may accuse bold gardens of excess, but they earn a "Wow!" from others.

great combinations: magnificent magenta

Daring gardeners savor magenta's good vibrations and discover endless ways to contrast one of the boldest of the bold colors for stunning combinations, such as:

- magenta coneflower with silver artemisia
- hot pink English primrose with chocolate-leaf bergenia
- magenta cosmos with purplish bronze fennel
- lime green euphorbia with magenta-flower zinnia
- a deep pink rose with cinnamon-hue plume poppy
- magenta sweet William with burgundy astilbe
- magenta 'Ann Folkard' geranium with golden orange daylily

no-brakes borders

above: A perennial border of bright delphinium, verbascum, *Anchusa azurea* 'Loddon Royalist', foxglove, and Maltese cross *(Lychnis chalcedonica)* appears beautifully balanced because all the flower colors register equal intensity.

impromptu palette

right: A mix of annual meadow flowers, including hot pink cosmos, striped mallow, blue bachelor's button, red flax, and yellow-and-burgundy coreopsis, displays a rich contrast of primary colors.

bold

go for the bold

Bold garden designs take a fresh look at color and its capabilities. They dare to stretch color to extremes. The hottest pink juxtaposes with golden orange. Deep velvety purple pairs with vibrant yellow. Scarlet ignites when standing next to orange or magenta. A palette of rich, saturated hues dazzles the viewer from dawn to dusk.

The bold garden relies on color celebrities of equal intensity, used in dramatic vignettes. Give a brilliant pair the limelight by placing them front row center in the border, and then repeat the colors in the background, creating an echo of the original color match.

To discover a good match, get close and look at the whole blossom. No flower has an absolute single-color affiliation. Striping, patches, sheens, stamens, undertones, or throat all contribute to the flower's petal palette. One or more of these shades may harmonize with a likely partner. Also consider how the flower petals change color as they unfurl, then fade. Some roses may turn three or four different hues from bud to full bloom that could suggest color partners.

Plant shapes and bloom times also play a role in bold matches. A marriage of unusual forms creates major chemistry. For example, *Angelica archangelica* towers in a shade garden and frolics spiritedly with the large, dark leaves and bright flowers of ligularia and gooseneck loosestrife.

partners that pop

right: **Blossoms of 'Purple Splendor' rhododendron and neon yellow perennial Iceland poppy would seem a jarring combination in an ordinary palette. But this bold design reaps the glowing payoffs of pairing yellow and purple—classically complementary. Both bloom in early spring.**

glowing pair

below: **The ember glow of 'Westerland' rose appears more luscious next to 'Wargrave Pink' geranium. A hardy Floribunda rose, 'Westerland' bears blooms that fade to peach, then to pink as they open, eventually almost matching the perennial geranium.**

Bold matches are limited only by the variety of flower colors available.

Success depends on timing. If you seek a color match and just can't find a flower partner that blooms at the same time, put foliage to work. The most breathtaking garden pairings often involve foliage understudies, not flower stars.

Plan your garden's bold color range for the intensity of light in its peak season. For instance, if plantings look their best in high summer, select the brightest colors possible so they won't fade in harsh sunlight. Tone down the color later by editing out plants or adding cooling white or silver plants as fillers among the brighter flowers.

bold

bold paint palette

Turn to perennials, shrubs, and bulbs to form your bold design's foundation. They'll give it stability with annual repeat performances.

Another bold approach involves a cast of thousands. Bright-flower summer annuals star in a mass planting that Victorian gardeners called bedding out; this bold scenario complements or contrasts colors. Or shades of the same color work in an analagous scheme. Mass plantings stop traffic with their sheer intensity of color. This type of bold garden requires lots of maintenance: fertilizing, watering, and removal of faded blooms keep the color showstopping.

Meadows result from nature's improvised mass plantings. Many a happy color accident happens when annual wildflowers mingle and turn up in unanticipated pairings. Predetermine the boldness of your meadow's color scheme by blending the seeds of your favorite hot hues. The meadow will perpetuate your brilliant scheme yearly by self-seeding.

Once you've got the knack of gardening boldly, surround yourself with color, overhead and all around. Think vertical and horizontal. Turn to trellises and arbors to raise the colors to new levels.

Gardens alone don't always instigate a bold design. Your color adventure may begin with a house color or an arbor painted in a favorite

south-of-the-border spice

above right: **The tropical leaves and volcanic blooms of cannas epitomize bold. Annual marigolds in a similar hot spectrum carry the brazen color scheme to the border's front. Choose cannas with striped foliage and neon-color flowers for maximum shock value.**

bold and beautiful

Use bold colors to enliven a scene, but remember to practice a modicum of restraint. Consider these outstanding color matches:

- Pair 'Royal Purple' smokebush with copper tulips or red Oriental poppies.
- Combine pink 'Silver Cup' lavatera with orange California poppies.
- Mingle red and gold daylilies, dahlias, and marigolds.
- Pair 'Goldsturm' *Rudbeckia* and *Aster × frikartii* 'Monch'. Include lamb's-ears as a calming device for the glowing duo.
- Mix summer bulbs: purple alliums and orange foxtail lilies.
- Contrast orange and yellow calendulas with flowering kale.

hue that calls for a coordinated garden. There again, foliage may provide all the highlights needed to support a bright house exterior or a hardscape accent. For example, a garden design featuring a complementary flower color mixed with white or silver will hold its own next to a periwinkle blue or lemon-yellow house.

When you go for a bold look, consider more than the plants. A warm-color fence, arbor, or chair, painted a rich hue of terra-cotta, apricot, yellow, or blue, brings out the brilliance of nearby, well-matched flower hues.

fiery pinnacles

left: Massed plumes of gold, scarlet, and burgundy celosia, an annual bedding plant that thrives in summer heat, turn this border into red-hot real estate. Pink geraniums in the foreground take the tone down a notch.

garden color | **65**

pastel

lighter shade of pale

For sheer delight, just add white. It gives pastel hues their glow. Pale pinks, blues, lavenders, and yellows light up shady places. Illuminated flowers create islands of calm, soothing us with their petal-soft lullabies. In gloomy climates, pastels shine. Pastels offer visual refuge where the sun beats down relentlessly. Fresh and quiet, pastel gardens invite leisurely evening strolls and restful interludes.

perennial oasis
left: A free-flowing perennial border features an edge of fragrant lavender and phlox. Delphiniums and annual pink poppies also define the color scheme.

soft and scented
above: Catmint, campanula, verbena, and lamb's-ears weave soft pastels into the perfumed edge of a perennial bed.

whiter shades
opposite: Yarrow, catmint, lamb's-ears, and 'The Fairy' rose continue to glow as the sun goes down. Snapdragon and larkspur enhance the group.

pastel

painting with pastels

Pastels radiate most strongly in indirect light and on overcast days. Consider planting the subtle colors where the morning or evening light lingers. Swathes of pale-color flowers guide the way along a moonlit garden path. They brighten areas, such as a patio or deck, where you're likely to spend evening hours relaxing. Your palette can include more than flowers. The gleam of a pale tree trunk or silver leaves emanating light has just as much impact in a pastel garden's magic.

Against the backdrop of a brick wall or a dark, unpainted fence, pastel flowers gleam. They create a spotlight when planted around a focal point in the garden, such as statuary or a fountain, especially when viewed from a distance.

quiet corner
above right: An understated blend of catmint, chamomile, salvia, and rose provides a relaxing spot to savor the aroma of herbs.

spring scenario
right: Spring and pastel color schemes seem to go together. The perennial groundcover *Phlox divaricata,* composes a pleasing complementary scheme with the flowering bulbs *Narcissus* 'Thalia' and a yellow jonquil.

An entire contingent of peacemaking pastel colors tends to appear tepid when planted together. Add a little visual friction in the form of contrasting colors, along with framing greens and silvers, to separate the pastel shades.

Pastel flowers often offer alluring fragrance. Many flaunt sweet scents that announce the flowers' availability to insect and bat pollinators. Add pale-color roses, lilacs, magnolias, and honeysuckle to your garden schemes and enjoy their perfume as you stroll through the garden.

desert cool
left: Three sturdy perennials for desert locales boast long-lasting color, including the 'Desert Sun' palo verde tree, *Agave americana,* and Mexican primrose (a groundcover).

foliage

the essential leaf

Raindrop diamonds glimmer on a crinkled lady's mantle leaf. Silver foliage flutters along Russian olive branches. Emerging heather growth glows lime green.

Foliage has an essential and complex function in the plant world. It converts sunlight to life-sustaining sugars. In garden design, leaves assume equally important roles. They prolong a border's attractions through the season, giving it depth, flow, and personality. Whereas flash-in-the-pan flowers display vibrant colors timed to guide inbound pollinators, leaves put on a longer-running show.

Leaves build architecture. Used as hedging, groundcover, background, or striking specimen, foliage defines garden contours and skylines.

In fact, a planting limited to green palettes fascinates as much as a floor show of flamboyant blooms. Of all colors, green is viewed and perceived most easily. Using various shades of green only and interweaving delicate, airy foliage with coarser leaves creates an impressive tapestry that's easy on the eyes. In an all-green garden, a single plant with bold, dramatic foliage assumes the spotlight where flowers would usually stand. It has equal impact.

edible ornamentals
above: In the vegetable garden, contrasting green and burgundy leaf lettuces provide both spring highlights and harvests.

textured collage
right: Fine-texture sedum, thyme, and artemisia combine with juniper on a dry, sunny site.

foliar finery
opposite: A shady border gleams with skillfully composed silver fern, hosta, euphorbia, and columbine.

foliage

uncommon greenery

As if green's foliar offerings weren't riches enough, leaf hues span the entire spectrum. Foliage artists can dabble in shades from the smoky black of mondo grass (*Ophiopogon 'Nigrescens'*) and snake root (*Cimicifuga racemosa*) to the ghostly silver–white of *Artemisia lactiflora* and *Eryngium*. Purple, red, blue, silver, and golden foliage all supply pigments for composing vibrant garden masterpieces. Color-splattered leaves, such as those found in coleus and tovara, match almost any other leaf or flower color. Many plants also have contrasting leaf veins that coordinate with other foliage colors.

Every foliar hue has a special effect in the border. Green calms and soothes, which is why gardens designed mainly with greens offer welcome relief in urban settings and meditational refuges such as Japanese tea gardens. Blue and blue–green foliage, found in fescue and oat grass, create a cool

dappled drama

above right: In this green-and-cream scheme, dark, reddish, and rippled greens in the forms of geranium, *Euphorbia* × *martinii*, and hosta have even more impact next to variegated tovara.

no-bloom bouquet

right: *Oxalis*, or wood sorrel, oak fern, and *Heuchera* 'Palace Purple' with Hinoki false cypress in the upper right corner create a symphony of shapes.

and elegant link to other colors in a garden. Blue leaves mixed with purple-leaf plants and magenta flowers look spectacular.

Purple and burgundy foliage anchor garden borders, giving them solidity. The warm reds in coleus, maple trees, and ornamental grasses such as *Miscanthus* raise the pulse of foliar compositions with excitement and drama. Yellows have the same uplifting effect as sunshine in the border.

Gray and silvery gray foliage play magic leaf tricks. Although gray is a neutral mix of other colors, it reflects tints of complementary color partners. Next to red, it becomes slightly green. Paired with violet, it appears yellowed. Grays placed near orange have a blue tinge.

leaves afire
above: A tender annual, coleus inflames containers and beds with a color range from bronze and gold to purple and lime green. It grows indoors as a houseplant over the winter.

swirls and stars
left: Its swirling heads of chartreuse flower bracts make perennial *Euphorbia* × *martinii* a harmonious foliage partner for a bordeaux-color Japanese maple tree. These plants thrive in semishaded, moist soil.

foliage

preserve the pattern

Speckled, striped, or margined, multicolor leaf patterns serve up a little something different on the foliage color menu. Two-tone flowers are bicolored, whereas patterned leaves are variegated. The most common variegations express themselves in cream-, yellow-, or white-and-green foliage. Other, rarer, color patterns include the silver streaks in *Heuchera, Tiarella, Pulmonaria,* and *Lamium* leaves, as well as the rainbow splatters found in Japanese maple hybrids, leucothoe, and other plants.

Vegetable leaves also display wildly variegated colors. Be sure to include red-speckle leaf lettuces, the frosted blue-green and lavender found in ornamental kale and cabbage, plus 'Rainbow' chard in your foliar palette of special effects.

Overall, variegated plants lighten and refresh a border, especially when blending green and white or green and cream. Plants naturally develop multicolor leaf mutations; then plant breeders discover, preserve, and copy them. Due to the instability in a hybrid's genetic makeup, it takes extra effort to help these plants thrive in the garden and sustain their showy leaves. Adequate fertilizer and plenty of sunlight preserve the showy foliage. Cut off flower stalks of variegated plants, such as polka-dot plant (*Hypoestes*), coleus, lamb's-ears, ornamental cabbage, flowering kale, lettuce, and basil, to ensure leaf vigor and continuous color.

glowing foliage

right: A variegated euphorbia pairs with 'Royal Cloak' purple barberry and chartreuse-leaf *Geranium sinense* in a hardy planting that furnishes almost year-round color.

radiant tapestry

left: A planting of perennial variegated golden ribbon grass, purple-leaf coral bells, and bergenia radiates with purple and gold-tone harmonies. The design works well as a front-of-the-border display or by providing foliar footlights under trees.

taking a shine to shade

below left: Silver sets the tone for this low-growing mélange of gray-green perennials, including *Pulmonaria, Anthriscus sylvestris* 'Ravens Wing', and *Arabis caucasica,* or rockcress. White florets of the *Arabis* and *Anthriscus* pose dainty counterpoints to the foliage.

multipurpose herb

below: The aromatic leaves of 'Tricolor' sage have culinary uses, and the plant edges flower beds with ornamental highlights.

foliage

a garden gold rush

You might associate yellow flowers with the sunny peak of summer, but golden foliage imparts instant warmth to a landscape year-round. Especially valuable in regions dominated by cloudy skies and diffused light, gold-leaf plants supply the missing sunshine. Shady areas, a frequent challenge in mature landscapes, take on a glow with golden foliage. You have many options when it comes to painting the border gold. The gold-tone leaf has become a focus in recent breeding and gilds everything from groundcovers and vines to trees.

Most foliage shows a hint of gold when first emerging in spring. Most tree and shrub foliage turns to burnished gold, prompted by fall frosts. Conifers, including *Chamaecyparis*, wear winter cloaks of gold-tinged green.

Other gold nugget plants include the most popular ornamental grasses for shade, *Hakonechloa macra* 'Aureola' and sedges. Are you bold enough for bamboo? Consider the 'Golden Goddess' and yellow-groove bamboos.

Pale gold and green-and-gold variegated hostas, reportedly more tolerant of sun, include 'Frances Williams' and 'Gold Standard'. Gold-splashed varieties of ligularia, a large-leaf perennial, offer other options for shade. Among vines, 'Gold Net' variegated honeysuckle goes airborne with golden foliage. Low to the ground, golden creeping Jenny and *Veronica repens* fill in gaps with their sunshine.

rivers of gold

right: In this colorful composition of 'Bowles Golden' tufted sedge, *Anthriscus* 'Ravens Wing', 'Aurea' barberry, variegated hosta, and 'Negrita' purple tulips, blooms provide contrast rather than focus. This perennial painting repeats itself each spring.

golden spikes

above: Gold-digging plants, such as variegated moor grass *(Molinia caerulea* 'Variegata'), 'Norton's Gold' oregano, and 'Aurea' barberry, will glow in just about any type of soil. A full-sun exposure enhances their gold coloration.

spend gold wisely

All that glitters doesn't necessarily pan out in a garden's design. Here are some locations where gold plants will pay high dividends:

- As an underplanting around trees and shrubs in shady areas.
- Contrasting and highlighting purple-leaf perennials and shrubs.
- Mingling with silver-variegated plants such as lungwort. Gray leaves cast a violet glow over gold and soften its impact.
- Blending with yellow- and green-variegated leaves, gold foliage looks as pretty and prominent as soft-yellow flowers.

tropical

touch of the tropics

Anything is possible when horticultural tradewinds bring adventurous plants to your yard. Banana leaves rise on the prairie; plumeria thrives in Iowa. Tropicalissimo warms the blood and the border with plant fantasies come true.

Dramatic structure and colors tip a garden's design into the tropical zone. The tiger-stripe foliage of a canna, and the vibrant lime, pink, and purple of coleus leaves, put the fun back in gardening. Victorian-era gardens popularized summer beds where circus-color menageries of exotic plants romped. Tropical plants seem at home in any climate. When the sun heats up, their growth accelerates into junglelike luxuriance.

hot and cold

above right: Sedum 'Mohrchen', with its rosy brown flowers and chocolatey stems, colors a perennial vignette with purple fleabane *(Erigeron karvinskianus)* that's tropical in flavor but hardy in cold climates.

tropical punch

right: In mai tai colors, *Dahlia* 'Simplicity' and *Alstroemeria* 'Beatrix' warm the border with summer flowers. In cold climates, dig up their tubers after the first frost and store them indoors through the winter.

jungle flora

opposite: A flock of flamingo-like striped cannas brings this perennial border into bold focus. Tropical touches include cape fuchsia, nicotiana, and fiery-flower potentilla and crocosmia. Butterfly bush, meadow rue, purple sage, lysimachia, and lady's mantle blend cooling touches of lavender and chartreuse.

foliage fever

Savvy gardeners value many tropical natives for their flamboyant foliage. Coleus, an annual in most North American climates, offers hundreds of varieties in shades of kiwi green, magenta, gold, burgundy, and white. Sun-tolerant varieties with thicker leaves have recently debuted.

Cannas, grown from rhizomes, sport bold leaves often striped in gold and topped with bright red, orange, yellow, or pink flowers. Another tuberous plant, caladium, develops arrowhead-shape leaves in pink, red, and green. Angel-wing and Rex begonias also add speckled and striped foliage to the tropical palette. Elephant's ear (*Colocasia*) contributes massive, lofty leaves in deep purple, gold, or green.

The unusual blooms of flowering plants from the tropics of Africa and South America, when

captivating coleus
below: **Like many tropicals, coleus responds well to an occasional deadheading. Pinch off their lavender flower spikes for a continuously showy crop of leaves.**

planted in borders or containers, form delicate contrasts against flamboyant leaves. Abutilon's inverted bell flowers attract hummingbirds by the droves, as do the trumpet blooms of *Phygelius* (cape fuchsia). *Brugmansia*, or angel's trumpet, boasts dramatic flowers with a sweet fragrance. Overwinter these torrid-zone plants indoors.

Hot oranges, reds, and yellows for painting tropical palettes come from nasturtium and Mexican sunflower *(Tithonia)*. Annual and perennial salvias supply blues, reds, and purples. Summer bulbs that also fit the tropical motif include crocosmia, dahlia, and *Eucomis*, or pineapple lily.

tropical's subtle side
left: Melianthus major, **or honey bush, poses with golden elephant's ear and 'Fascination' dahlia. It grows as an annual in cold climates.**

tiger tale
left: **Growing to an imposing 6 feet, 'Bengal Tiger' (also known as 'Praetoria') is one of the showiest cannas, with apricot-orange flowers appearing successively from midsummer to the first frost. Potting summer-flowering tubers and bulbs keeps them portable and easy to move indoors to overwinter.**

tropical illusions

The best-kept secret about tropical gardens is that not all the players need hail from exotic locales. Think large and dramatic foliage plus bold color, and you'll end up with hundreds of plants that are growable in your garden all year despite long, cold winters. Glossy groundcovers with a lush habit include hardy arums and asarums. You can't beat *Acanthus*, *Gunnera*, or *Rheum* for leafy architecture, and all these perennials survive cold winters. The imposing leaves of catalpa and magnolia trees have a tropical feel, yet they're quite hardy. Dutchman's pipe, trumpet vine, and hardy passionflower display a junglelike vigor, and the vast bamboo and fern families number several cold-hardy species in their ranks.

Among succulents, sedum, sempervivum, yucca, and prickly pear cactus can weather cold winters. *Melianthus*, a fringed silvery shrub from mountainous Africa, ranks high on the list of tropical wannabes. It has an imposing structure and a crowd-pleasing color that makes it an outstanding companion plant. New Zealand flax (*Phormium*) has multicolor straplike leaves that make good focal points in tropical-theme borders. Some *Phormium* hybrids are hardy to Zone 7.

After the final frost in spring, plant showy annuals to fill gaps in a tropical-look garden. Use castor bean, plume poppy, and cleome for striking height or form. Annual vines grown from seed,

sassy dancers
right: **Think of potted tropicals as living flower arrangements or the Carmen Mirandas of containers. Weekly feeding and removal of spent flowers help keep coleus, caladium, petunia, lantana, pentas, and canna looking lush all summer.**

such as purple hyacinth bean, scarlet runner bean, or black-eyed Susan vine, rise up quickly and entwine structures in junglelike lushness.

Houseplants that have languished on the windowsill all winter can also be exported to add color to tropical borders. Hibiscus, palm, and others bring Hawaiian-shirt shades and shapes into temperate gardens. Make an easy fall transition to indoors by keeping a group of potted houseplants on the patio or deck, or gather them in a corner of the garden that offers late-day shade.

tropical leaf motif

left: **A potted garden showcases assorted wavy foliage of elephant's ear and caladium punctuated by knobs of lavender allium and green amaranth spikes. All except the annual amaranth are bulbs to be saved for the next year's planting.**

quick-and-easy tropical decor

- String up a hammock or sky chairs in place of traditional loungers. Choose rattan, wicker, or bamboo furniture.
- Use large-print floral fabrics in bright colors for a tablecloth, napkins, cushion covers, or a folding screen.
- Replace a standard patio umbrella with a *talapa* (a thatch reed umbrella designed to withstand harsh coastal conditions).
- Select bamboo as a building material for structures of all sorts, from plant supports and fencing to an arbor or a pergola.

color in the shade

shady propositions

The shade of established trees and tall buildings invites opportunities of shadowy splendor. Enjoy a colorful shade garden by choosing from a vast population of shade-loving perennials, annuals, and tropicals.

Container gardens make it easy to paint by number in the shade. Coleus, Persian shield (*Strobilanthes*), caladium, lisianthus, polka-dot plant, and ornamental sweet potato vine (*Ipomoea batatas*) take to the shady life with zeal, growing up and spilling over in no time. Mix them with the brilliant blooms of tuberous begonia, New Guinea impatiens, vinca, white or blue browallia, pentas, abutilon, and fuchsia to create memorable masterpieces that illuminate the shade.

Successful potted gardens often break the rules about who can live where. Sun lovers may thrive as temporary tenants in partial shade, especially if you meet their needs for heavy feeding and flower grooming. If plant colors start to flag, move the container to a sunnier spot.

One other rule made to be broken pertains to the pots themselves. In shade, colorful containers should stand out and be counted. Use roomy, bright-color vessels pierced with drainage holes to spotlight flashy, exotic plants.

made for shade

right: Tiered container plants stage a wall of blazing color on a shady deck. The gathering represents an annual who's-who of shady horticulture. Ornamental sweet potato vine, coleus, Persian shield, and New Guinea impatiens feature prominently with sun-loving zinnias and lantana.

color in the shade

shadow dancing

Shaded ground can glow with color from both flower and foliage gems. Start by layering shades of green, and place a variegated or yellow-leaf plant at the center of a grouping. Frame a green-and-white hosta, for example, with a background of silvery ferns. Take a tip from Asian gardens by incorporating one flowering plant, such as camellia or rhododendron, as a seasonal accent in a sea of tranquil green.

Just a few of the colorful and textural foliage options for shade include *Aquilegia, Dicentra,* or *Nandina* for delicacy; boxwood, euonymus, or daphne for highlights; *Acanthus,* hellebore, and gunnera for structure; and *Lamium, Pulmonaria,* and *Houttuynia* for contrast. Employ fine-texture ivies, *Schizanthus,* and climbing hydrangea to ascend the walls, adding extra dimensions of green, silver, and white. Climbing bleeding heart, *Dicentra scandens,* bears dainty yellow flowers in partial shade.

Ornamental grasses illuminate and soften semishady garden edges, spilling over walkways. Sedges, golden hakone grass, and feather reed grass all tolerate shady locales.

Hardscaping also helps illuminate shady areas. Walkways and stepping-stones in pale flagstone or concrete bring a gleam to shadowy paths. Water features, mirrors, and reflective gazing balls open up shaded areas, adding flashes of brilliance.

lighten up
right: Light-color flowers, foliage, and pavers make this dim enclosure appear warm and expansive. The fountain and pool reflect a bit of light too.

fantastic footlight

left: A gazing ball catches and throws back sunlight, magically opening a shady area in a double exposure. Salvia spikes form a flattering frame for the silver sphere.

texture trove

below left: A montage of shade-thriving perennials includes ground-carpeting *Pulmonaria*, *Pachysandra*, columbine, hosta, and silver fern.

1,000-watt color in the shade

- Supplement garden color with large pots of brilliant blooms (petunia, begonia) and foliage (caladium, coleus).
- Concentrate on warm and vivid contrasts in your shady color scheme, especially reds and burgundies with yellow and chartreuse.
- Furnish a shady corner with chairs, pots, or structures painted a glowing color.
- Include reflective features, such as light–tone concrete statuary, a fountain, or a small pool of water.
- Use ground lighting to set the place aglow after sunset. Dangle lanterns in trees.

garden color | **87**

monochromatic

one-on-one

Single-color gardens show as much boldness and flair as the most elaborately matched schemes. A one-color strategy frees you to master the brushstrokes of form and texture. It also allows enough elbow room to explore a single-color palette's potential in pale and deep shades.

Consider green, for example; it doesn't fatigue the eye. It offers an endlessly varying palette, from true green, gray-green, and blue-green to purple-green and yellow-green. Each has a different impact.

In small, all-green spaces, paint with plenty of blue-green plants. Blue-tint leaves have the same deepening effect as blue flowers. Blue hostas and Solomon's seal visually widen shady areas with their broad leaves. Rue, thalictrum, and *Rosa glauca* weave lacy texture into all-green gardens.

Color contrasts in a monochromatic garden rouse a simple palette and make it sing. Purple-green looks dramatic when rubbing elbows with yellow-green, for example. Blend pools of true green or silvery green in between.

green unlimited

right and *below:* **This pond garden has a sweeping vista in a palette of greens. The statue, trellis, and rocks add contrasting textures.**

plant list

1 boxwood
2 nandina
3 blue oat grass
4 japanese privet
5 siberian iris
6 calla lily
7 rose
8 armeria

monochromatic

illuminating white

Turn a garden into a classic, using a palette of white. Widely available in flowers, foliage, and garden decor, white projects a refreshing clarity. Paint with white to expand your garden's visual boundaries just as you would brush on white to enlarge interior rooms. Dull or shady areas, especially, benefit from white's sparkle.

Include any variation of white, from buff to silver, to give your white garden interest beyond the pale. Light pastel colors blend well too, so highlight white with pale peach, yellow, lavender, and pink. In an all-white garden, texture becomes all important in establishing individual plant identities. Combine thick, satiny petals with sheer

evening glow

above right: Gleaming candlelight and glowing annual *Zinnia angustifolia* team up with ribbon grass and artemisia to illuminate a gravel path.

summer whites

right: An all-white arrangement of phlox, hydrangea, baby's breath, and 'Fair Bianca' rose, accented with silver lamb's-ears, reaches its flowering peak in midsummer but looks fresh and tranquil all season. The arbor adds architectural white.

ones; set off large, showy blooms by framing them with feathery flowers or foliage.

All-white gardens shine as the sun goes down. Place a fragrant white border where it will captivate at twilight. Some white fragrant bloomers to place along paths and lean against arbors include peonies, nicotiana, moonflowers, phlox, and lilies. Include jasmine or stephanotis in warm climates.

Garden elements reflect the same glow as white plantings. Pale-color gravel, stepping-stones, arbors, and picket fences put a permanent luster on white gardens.

shade paint
left: **Like white paint indoors, white wood in a dark garden corner creates a sense of space. Crisp white clematis and variegated bishop's weed *(Aegopodium)* enhance the effect.**

monochromatic

heat waves

Florists and gardeners share this successful technique: An arrangement composed around a single color epitomizes elegance. Monochromatic plantings designed from the spectrum's warm side leave memorable impressions.

Textural interplay heightens the drama of a one-color garden. The bold trumpets of orange daylilies, for example, dance bloom to bloom with delicate plumes of pale peach astilbe and glowing wands of 'Lucifer' crocosmia. Strategic plant location also heightens the impact of monochromes. Place loose or open-branched plants toward the border front to allow a view through of more substantial flowers beyond. This down-in-front framing strategy helps create the same sense of suspense and depth as a bend in the path or a long view through an arbor.

Another design technique involves planting a bed of annuals in monochromatic bands. Beds of multicolor annuals can confuse rather than compel. If limited to a single color and specific varieties, however, the planting has stronger impact.

Light intensity also heightens monochrome drama. An all-yellow border dazzles under softly lit, overcast skies or when located in a shady nook. Orange or red schemes look stunning poised against a west-facing view, where the sinking sun backlights them with a fiery aura.

light a fire

right: **A rich-hue band of coleus spreads like fire across the border and reflects the daylilies' colors. The warm-color scheme enlivens the neutral-tone house.**

golden glow

left: A sunny border puts yellow's synergy to work by combining daylilies, heliopsis, and coreopsis. Yellow corydalis, trollius, and golden hosta offer options for a border in the shade.

peachy pizzazz

below: A molten flow of orange dahlias, nasturtium, rose, and salpiglossis, contrasted with chartreuse euphorbia and white feverfew, flatters the warm tones of the brick border edging.

monochromatic

purple majesty

Purple reigns supreme in the garden. The color of cabbages and kings plants peace between louder colors and deserves garden homage to its quiet tones. An all-purple or all-lavender garden would appear downright melancholy. But various purple hues, mingled with silver or gold foliage and amplified with red or orange counterpoints, would emanate luminous splendor.

Make a purple planting more dynamic by playing every note in the purple range: violet, mauve, periwinkle, deep reddish purple, and purplish black. Give lavender the role of blender, as in multicolor gardens.

Once you've established a purple foundation, add contrasts. Surround purple plants with lighter silver and brighter gold to keep them in focus. Golden cultivars of conifers, flowering shrubs, and

autumn mists

above right: Asters, phlox, grasses, and woolly lamb's-ears seem to float above the ground, but the solid green of the bergenia leaves anchors the plantings.

quiet scene

right: The lavender of catmint and *Verbena bonariensis* below a red Japanese maple would look somber without the softening effect of lamb's-ears and golden hops. The lone pink poppy adds a lighthearted note.

ornamental grasses stand out next to purple plants. Mingle purple smokebush and a purple-flowering *Buddleia* with a golden elderberry or 'Golden Sword' *Yucca flaccida.*

Silver companions shine in the presence of purple and bring out its mysterious side. Pair lamb's-ears with aster, artemisia with a lavender rose, and autumn crocus with silvery blue fescue to create ethereal vignettes.

Avoid monotony in purple schemes by weaving in one emphatic color. Use just a few plants that accent the flower centers of purple blooms or the veining of purple leaves. A shout of fiery red or flashes of brilliant orange cast purple in a flattering light. One hot pink spotlight in a contrasting shape also works as the exclamation point in an all-purple statement.

purple pleasers

- groundcovers: 'Burgundy Glow' *Ajuga*
- tropicals: 'Blackie' ornamental sweet potato vine, lantana, coleus, Persian shield
- perennials: 'Vera Jameson' sedum
- herbs: 'Purpureum' bronze fennel, 'Dark Opal' basil, 'Berggarten' sage, perilla
- vegetables: eggplant, 'Lollo Rosso' lettuce, 'Royal Burgundy' bush beans, 'Purple Passion' asparagus, 'Ruby Perfection' cabbage

fall sunset scheme
left: Ageratum 'Blue Horizon', cosmos, and aster show the luminiscent quality of lavender with colorful support from the grenadine-color chrysanthemum.

two-color

white weddings

Combined with any color, white has the impact of a mint sprig in lemonade: It adds an edge of refreshing crispness. White's chameleon-like nature also makes it the color companion valued most in the garden. Next to warm yellows and reds, white softens. With cool blue and purple, it appears frosty and defined. Free from color, white assumes whatever tint stands next to it.

Drifts of white in a red-hot border lower the temperature. A red and white scheme strikes a balance between excitement and relaxation. For a fresh-faced look, pair yellow or orange flowers with white blooms that have warm-color centers.

Planted next to recessive blue flowers or foliage, white shines like a lightbulb in bloom, yet the overall effect is quiet and harmonious. Whites drawn from either variegated foliage or flowers become highlights when interspersed among green, particularly in a shady setting. Combined with pink, lavender, or silver, white appears enchanting. White roses peeking out among lavender phlox, or lavender clematis draped on a white arbor, look stunning at twilight.

shades of nightfall

right: **Oakleaf hydrangea, snapdragon, and sweet alyssum star in this circular garden, but nuances of lavender scabiosa, campanula, delphinium, and salvia soften the potential glare of the mostly-white scene.**

blue and white classic

opposite: **White flowers would ordinarily fade into a white house, but the peegee hydrangea outshines a blue spruce standard, a dwarf Alberta spruce, blue salvia, and variegated plectranthus.**

two-color

midas touches

When yellow joins other flower colors, the scene invariably lightens and brightens. Yellow boosts the border with the visual equivalent of laughter. It shimmers in shady places.

Purple tones, from purplish green to lavender, respond warmly to a yellow partner. Bright spring yellows frequently pair up with purple and blue blooms. But what about a late-spring follow-up act of yellow peonies (*Paeonia lutea*) with purple-leaf rhododendrons; lavender irises and gold *Veronica repens*; or 'Baggesen's Gold' honeysuckle and hardy ginger (*Roscoea purpurea*)?

Use yellow shrubs as ornamental highlights in flower borders. They'll add spark to mellow monochromes of purple or pink. Many gardeners greet the spring with bright yellow forsythia, but other shrubs spread wonderful buttery color in plantings. For shade, *Kerria japonica* bears single or double popcorn flowers of pure gold against vivid green stems. *Kirengeshoma*, a large perennial, and *Rhododendron luteum* twinkle with pale yellow flowers, while mahonia glistens with sprays of bright yellow. In sunny gardens, witch hazel and broom (*Cytisus*) flower in early spring. Golden-leaf varieties of weigela, elderberry, caryopteris, and barberry enhance borders with their glow.

Yellow and white form a winning combination that glows dramatically when reflected in water.

border light

right: Yellow daylilies and coreopsis add sparkle to a palette of purples, including smokebush, coneflower, petunia, and phlox. The scheme would appear muddy without yellow's light and cheerful touch.

A midsummer border could pair fragrant yellow-throated *Lilium regale* and 'Stella de Oro' daylily, or white astilbe and a gold-variegated ornamental grass. By adding 'Goldfinch' goldenrod or 'Garden Sun' helenium and white mums, the gold and white show lasts through the fall.

Many daisylike yellow flowers provide late-summer color. Sustain the sunshine of coreopsis, helenium, and black-eyed Susan by snipping off faded flowers after their first bloom. A second flowering soon follows.

faces in the clouds
below: **A mass of purples and yellows visually softens the bronze sundial. Two-tone pansies emanate personality, as lavender and lady's mantle form clouds of summer color.**

two-color

red-hot matches

Reds highlight otherwise subdued colors so they'll be noticed. Warm colors intensify when stationed next to red. Cool classics, such as green and white, suddenly look fresh and sparkling when a dash of red is applied among them.

Green, especially, gains vibrancy in the company of its complement: red. The green-and-red leaves of caladium or *Euphorbia × martinii* look spectacular combined with deep red flowers, including tuberous begonia, fuchsia, and *Lobelia cardinalis.* Unusual green flowers, such as hellebore or bells of Ireland, go well with reddish-foliage plants. Rich reds, found in roses and peonies, create beautiful relationships with the chartreuse leaves and flowers of lady's mantle or cushion spurge. Any green or chartreuse shrub glows in the company of a red Japanese maple.

Red and yellow make a happy blend of two warm temperaments. Such strong colors should register equal intensity to combine successfully, golden yellow with bright red, for example. When yellow flowers sport contrasting red centers or markings, such as daylilies, tulips, *Coreopsis tinctoria,* gaillardia, and helenium, the bond grows even stronger.

Red adds a pulse to all-white plantings. White and red roses provide a classic look among dark green foliage. A ribbon of white mums winding around a fall-reddened tree or shrub looks exquisite. Likewise, Japanese blood grass mixing with 'Snowbank' boltonia or white asters create a stellar combination.

formal with a flair

right: **Bands of red impatiens and gladiolas, plus other red accents, enliven a formal scheme.**

dynamic duets

- deep blue with peach: delphinium and pale peach Oriental poppy
- silver-blue and ruby red: blue spruce entwined with 'Niobe' clematis
- burgundy flowers and silver foliage: dahlias planted around cardoon
- red and gold: *Astrantia* paired with sedge
- deep purple and pale yellow: purple coleus with trailing light–yellow lantana
- orange with buff: 'Paprika' yarrow and *Stipa tenuissima* (an ornamental grass)

spicy hot

below: A timber-edge bed warms to a spring bulb-and-annual medley of yellow and red ranunculus, Temari verbena, calendula, geranium, stock, Dutch iris, and white creeping zinnia.

two-color

two-part harmonies

Side by side on the color wheel, reds and oranges also bond in the border. To ensure compatibility, select reds that run to warm crimson rather than cool burgundy. Red flax or poppies mingled with orange butterfly weed creates jewel-like effects in a meadow garden setting. A mix of red and peach dahlias sizzles in a hot-weather color scheme, especially if the 'Bishop of Llandaff' dahlia, with its chocolate-color foliage, fills the red role. 'Lady in Red' annual salvia, paired with nasturtiums and 'Peaches 'n' Cream' verbena, strikes equally warm notes up front in the border or arranged in a pot.

Pink and white plantings also radiate warmth, but with pastel overtones. Both colors get along with any other. Paired with each other, however, the combo is as delicious as strawberries and cream. Soft, satiny pink 'Bonica' roses spilling over a white picket fence couldn't ask for any better company than pink-and-white alstroemeria, magenta penstemon, and the starry white counterpoint of *Leucanthemum paludosum*.

For a slightly warmer look, introduce yellow to your favorite deep pink flowers. Gold foliage provides the least intrusive way to play up the color chemistry. Use *Helichrysum* 'Limelight' to set off magenta petunias, for instance. Rosy phlox and pink coneflowers create striking pairs with golden-flower perennials.

rosy rabbit refuge

right: Purples and pinks hit it off in a border filled with geranium, lobelia, sweet alyssum, barberry, daisy, and 'The Fairy' rose. Golden arborvitae focal points, along with the bold foliage of strawberry, sedum, and others, keep the rosy scene from appearing too precious.

sizzling slope

below: **Cascades of annual nasturtiums and million bells, plus impatiens, dahlias, and *Cuphea*, warm the brick walls of a terraced garden with hot points of color. The barberry below and pale climbing rose above contribute structure. Green pots and foliage provide continuity among the spice-color flowers.**

Closely related on the color wheel, pink and purple make a successful team in the garden. Annual *Salvia viridis* furnishes both colors on spiky stalks. Purple larkspur pairs beautifully with pink poppies, and lisianthus goes with pink 'Garden Bride' baby's breath. Violet clematis and pink roses paint a rich, two-tone portrait. Purple basil makes a stunning foliage filler in a bed of pink blooms. An early-spring scene features pink creeping phlox and purplish-blue forget-me-not. Pink autumn crocus and purple-bronze *Ajuga* combine for fall.

Make purple pop by adding an orange partner, such as tall zinnias accompanying 'Purple Rain' salvia, or match blooms of lavender bellflower with coral 'Elfin Pink' penstemon.

trios

three's company

The whole is greater than the sum of its parts. This adage proves true in the garden where pairs of companionable plants are common. But whereas two are good, three can be better.

When a three-part color harmony relies solely on flowers, its timing must be in sync. Group three plants that should bloom about the same time in the season to make an effective trio. A late-spring design could include Oriental poppy, iris, and delphinium. Plan late-blooming replacements and extend the trio into midsummer. Let blue larkspur take over for the iris and add annual poppies to fill in after the Oriental poppy foliage fades.

What's the easiest way to start thinking in threes? Take a favorite flowering shrub, such as a rose or a long-blooming perennial, then showcase it with two foliage partners. Select foliage for its shape but also for factors such as fall color and tones that pick up color in the flowers' petals, stamens, or markings. Many flowers have golden stamens, so gold foliage often makes a good partner for them.

thinking in threes

- Plant in threes. Practicing this old garden adage results in a fully mature-looking spread of one plant variety when adding new plantings.
- Decorate in threes. Choose one main color and add two accent colors to create a color scheme that plays on harmonies or contrasts.
- Accessorize in threes. Arrange colorful pots or other decorative elements in groups of three or five for the best results.

flower power

above: Subtle color paints this grouping of a 'New Dawn' rose, *Geranium pratense*, and *Euphorbia* 'Mrs. Robb's'. The geranium flowers early to midsummer; the rose blooms all summer. A favorite Climber, the rose grows up to 10 feet high and is hardy to Zone 5.

petal collage

right: Two perennials and 'Graham Thomas', a Shrub rose, combine in a trio of silky-petal pastels. The lavender *Campanula persicifolia*, or peach-leaf bellflower, flourishes in a sunny spot. Cut back the stems after the first bloom to encourage new shoots. Pink 'Proteus' clematis features double flowers and tolerates cold winters to Zone 4.

trios

triple treats

Triple the potential fragrance of roses by partnering them with small- and medium-height herbs. Versatile herbs possess aromatic appeal and they repel pests and soilborne diseases. Herbs also function as border edgers, perennial partners, and background choruses. Many of them have culinary uses too.

Sprays of bright-blue borage flowers and their prickly silver-green leaves add a glow to blooming companions. Borage makes a winning partner with peach and yellow roses. It grows easily and rapidly from seed.

Place a fine-texture haze of color behind brilliant flowers with angelica, bronze fennel, tarragon, or a taller artemisia, such as 'Silver King'. Add chartreuse highlights, especially among red or orange flowers, with dill or an arbor of golden hops. Artemisia, lavender, rosemary, and clary sage shine silver spotlights on white and pink or white and lavender combos.

For edging color and texture, rely on parsley, chives, sage (especially the purple and tricolor varieties), and globe basil. Creeping varieties of thyme and mint pave edges and walkways with shades of gold, purple, and green.

pink portrait
right: **'Earth Song', a Grandiflora rose, rises with fragrant dianthus and thyme at its feet. Foliage on the early-summer-blooming perennials stays attractive all summer. The rose bears double blooms and grows to 5 feet.**

terrific trio

left: Bee balm, lavender, and yarrow sustain
a colorful summer border of perennial herbs.
They also boast fragrance and a history as
herbal remedies. The plants dry well for wreath
making and other decorative uses.

easy threesie

below: Spanish lavender, purple sage, and
'Doone Valley' thyme form a striking and
aromatic group in hot sun and dry soil.
Lavandula stoechas flowers in early summer,
with hardiness to Zone 7.

garden color | **107**

trios

spring combos

Spring wears a mostly subdued color wardrobe, except for the bright yellow exultations of daffodils and forsythia. The season is typically depicted in soft pink, lavender, and blue. These three pastel colors work well together and separately when mixed with yellow–green, silver, and the white of blossoming fruit trees. In spring, flowering bulbs appear first, often wearing complementary shades of purple or lavender and yellow. The earliest perennials soon follow and become colorful coverups for fading bulb foliage. Plant coral bells, periwinkle, dianthus, columbine, cushion spurge, and lady's mantle over and around spring bulbs.

repeat performance

right: Count on this easy perennial trio to return early every summer: penstemon, cranesbill, and 'Blue Butterfly' delphinium.

bunches of blooms

above: Blue, pink, and purple bouquets of early-spring blooms include perennial *Phlox subulata*, forget-me-not, and annual *Viola cornuta*.

tantalizing trio

left: Plumes of astilbe mingle with *Dianthus barbatus* and columbine. Lady's mantle fills in the background. These perennials thrive in partial shade and organic-enriched soil.

garden color | **109**

trios

peak season

Summer favors a red-hot color scheme that stands up and shouts despite punishing heat. Beds and borders catch fire with golden yellows, searing reds, and volcanic oranges. When composing midsummer trios, always include at least one cooldown color to keep the fire under control. A splash of silver or dabs of white take the temperature down a notch. Calming pinks and blues also moderate hot colors.

hot cha-cha

right: **Annual red salvia, black-eyed Susan, and *Gaillardia* sizzle next to the cooling white of perennial Shasta daisies. Keep the daisies coming by removing faded flowers.**

butterflies are free

below: **Orange butterfly weed, *Aesclepias*, and yellow Asiatic lilies harmonize with spiky blue veronica. This midsummer combo attracts butterflies.**

Winning three-way garden partnerships combine red, white, and yellow or orange. Orange, yellow, and blue-theme borders prove that one cool tone plus two fiery allies can hit it off. Midsummer blues come from bachelor's button, campanula, delphinium, ageratum, and ladybells. Purple, gold, and silver reflect the sun's glory in a cooler, sophisticated scheme. Imagine the refreshing and reflective nature of a shady summer oasis painted green, white, and lavender or pink.

desert dazzlers

above: Desert spoon shrub, *Dasylirion wheeleri,* fans its silvery leaves in the midst of *Verbena rigida* and *Gaillardia.* Desert natives all, the three plants form a permanent perennial planting.

endless summer

left: The orange-gold blooms of perennial *Rudbeckia* would be an overwhelming radiant mass without the interspersed cool tones of lavender aster and lamb's-ears. The bursts of sunny color continue with a little help from the pruning shears to remove faded blooms.

garden color | **111**

trios

three parts foliage

When leaves play together in three-part harmony, the garden gains textural dimensions as well as colorful special effects. The soft ripple of grasses and the whorled pinwheels of euphorbias push the gardener's brushstrokes a step further into the complexities of shape and form.

Foliage eases the way to experimenting with color. Minus flower distractions, a collage of leaves clearly shows when color combinations work. Gather leaves from the plants you'd like to include in a garden vignette and arrange them next to one another on a sheet of paper. This will give you a compass bearing to follow with your garden's design. Add flowering plants last as seasonal accents among layers of ever-fascinating foliage.

Most foliage hues mingle well. Striking burgundy or purple leaves and showy variegated foliage substitute for flowers in a leafy garden. Gold goes well with purple, and silver adds a muted sparkle to the trio. Silver, gold, and yellow–green variegated foliage compose a gorgeous blend. A landscape dominated by purple and silver foliage suggests an aura of somber mystery lightened somewhat by a chartreuse or gold highlight.

silver streak

right: Dusty miller puts the spark into a planting of *Euphorbia wulfenii* and purple barberry. A tender annual, the dusty miller will need replacing the next season. Pluck off the flower spikes to encourage the showy foliage.

covering ground
above: A yellow and white perennial pair, *Alyssum saxatile* 'Citrinum' and snow-in-summer, gain another dimension with fine-texture blue oat grass.

purple haze
left: The shade's aglow when purple and yellow combine, as in this team of purple heuchera, variegated green-and-gold hosta, and the golden grass, *Hakonechloa*.

portable color

container combos

Potted gardens carry color quickly and conveniently to wherever it's needed. They also furnish dress rehearsals for a future in-the-ground garden. If you're contemplating color schemes for a full-fledged bed or border, first try them out by mixing colors and textures together in a pot.

Container gardens sustain colorful plantings over a long period with some simple guidelines. Start with a pot that's large enough to accommodate plant growth and expanding root systems. Professional garden designers recommend spacious containers of at least 12 inches in diameter or larger. Plan for a dense display of color, leaving only a few inches between each plant. Always give plants as healthy a start as possible with good-quality potting soil. An organic mix that includes a high humus content and balanced fertilizers gets color off to a fast start.

box punch
above: A wooden crate spills over with Persian shield, Algerian ivy, polka-dot plant, and caladium. The tender plants can live through the winter protected indoors.

potted paradise
right: Sweet-scented heliotrope mingles with fragrant nicotiana, cascading lobelia and ivy, soft yellow-green helichrysum, and spiky New Zealand flax. Only the flax lives past summer, in Zones 6 and warmer, with protection.

twist and shout
opposite: Towering, multicolor copperleaf makes a foil for swirls of candy pink petunias and chocolate-leaf ornamental sweet potato vines. The tender tropicals offer a long-lived option for warm, humid climates.

portable color

movable feasts

Potted gardens allow unlimited freedom when it comes to choosing what plants to mix and match. Opt for anything that can live temporarily in close quarters. Annuals mix with perennials. Ornamental grasses rub elbows with small trees or bulbs.

The same color harmonies that rule beautiful permanent gardens also apply to portable ones. Cool container schemes of blues and greens project tranquillity; reds, oranges, and yellows stir things up. Pinks and lavenders integrate separate pots into a unified look. Blue contrasted with yellow, or orange with purple, puts a potted garden in the spotlight. Include varying foliage for texture and to complement or contrast. Your containers will be within close-up view, where their vivid color details can be appreciated.

color where it counts

Container plantings put color at your garden decorating beck and call, especially where ground is limited or of poor quality.

- Cluster pots of shade-loving varieties around a tree.
- Place sturdy or low-growing windproof plants on a city terrace.
- Line a path with uniform pots or planted concrete blocks.
- Group colorful containers on a fire escape.
- Flank a front door or steps with symmetrical potted shrubs or small trees.
- Hang flat-back planters on a bare wall.

Well-balanced container gardens, whether in buckets, boxes, pots, urns, or troughs, all follow the zen of an artful flower arrangement. Design begins with scale. The tallest element stands in the center or slightly off to one side. It should be two and a half times the height of the container. Medium-size plants fill in around the center; short or cascading plants on the edges complete the design.

To plant a tropical-theme container, for example, set a canna, hibiscus, or dwarf banana plant in the middle and surround it with amaranth, caladium, nicotiana, or fuchsia. Add plumbago, lantana, or ornamental sweet potato vine as the cascading grand finale.

Start a naturalistic theme with a tall grass in dramatic colors, work in a few round-profile perennials, and then shorter annuals or herbs around the rim.

ripple effect

above: Succulents with intricately layered shapes thrive in this array of metal cauldrons and clay urns. The garden includes sempervivums and echeverias, desert natives that tolerate hot sun and dry conditions.

plant library

left: This vintage wooden magazine stand houses a brilliant collection of frost-tender coleus, impatiens, and verbena.

rust bucket

opposite: A rusty square bucket brims with an unexpected mix of houseplants and perennials, including tall *Cordyline terminalis* 'Red Sister', 'Moonbeam' coreopsis, variegated dense-flowered loosestrife *(Lysimachia)*, and the vining annual sweet potato 'Blackie'.

portable color

potted pleasures

Container gardens please the most when they're
unpredictable. Combine plants in odd numbers
of three, five, or seven to achieve unexpected,
asymmetrical art instead of rigid patterns. Plant
summer-flowering bulbs, perennials, and new
annual varieties for fun.

Use portable plantings as a visual extension
of your in-ground garden. Follow the same color
scheme and style to make a transition from plots
to pots. Does a plain wall or a long fence in your
garden beg for transformation? Decorate it with
hanging baskets planted in hues that bring the
background material to life. Stage potted plants
on stairs or a balcony to add high notes of
lushness and color.

The container itself becomes an integral element
in a potted garden. In the most striking container
gardens, a plant's silhouette matches that of its pot.
A rounded shrub or perennial fits best in a low
container that has slightly flared edges. A topiary
looks its most elegant in a tall, narrow pot
that suits its shape. A cascading plant makes an
impression when showcased in a wide-brim urn.

Traditional shapes in plastic, terra-cotta,
fiberglass, and lightweight styrene provide hospitable
plant lodgings, but unexpected containers turn
potted gardens into a party. Forays to garage sales,
flea markets, and thrift stores may turn up that

stepping up

right: Potted plants staggered on the stairway
create a brilliant transition from ground floor
to deck. Tuberous begonias, geraniums, lilies,
petunias, and eucomis (an elegant, summer-
flowering bulb) share the stage. Support the tall
lilies with an informal tripod of bamboo stakes.

chorus line

below: **A hanging garden of jewel-color annuals adorns a wall with living draperies. Geraniums, petunias, nasturtiums, and bidens all have flowing shapes well suited to basket growing. Remove faded flowers to extend the summer-long show.**

perfect vessel for a contained masterpiece. Buckets, wagons, wooden boxes, baskets, old chairs, and trunks offer plantable treasures. Limit your use of metal containers to shady areas, however, as metal conducts heat. Overheated plant roots cannot absorb water and will be permanently damaged. Line baskets and other containers you wish to protect with sheets of plastic stapled to the inside. Make a drainage hole or fill the bottom of the container with styrene packing material.

Found props also highlight potted gardens with whimsical touches. Miniature birdhouses on sticks, gracefully shaped branches, croquet mallets, tool heads, and other finds accessorize pots with creative color. They also make imaginative plant supports.

portable color: shallow bowl

zones	make it	skill
all	1 hour	easy

you will need

one 6-inch perennial aster

one 4-inch mum

one 4-inch variegated ivy

one 6-inch rock fern

one ornamental cabbage

one 6-inch sedum

one 16-inch-diameter terra-cotta bowl

scrap of window screen

soilless potting mix

autumn display

Most container color schemes need refreshment come early fall. This easy-to-put-together potted garden celebrates fall colors with a gathering of hardy plants in tones of green, lavender, magenta, and coral. Note how the gently sloped silhouette of the plantings flatters the low, wide bowl. The circular garden is designed to look good from any angle.

Most of the bowl garden's perennial plants, including the aster, mum, and rock fern, will settle permanently in the garden if planted before the first killing frost. The sedum lives on through the winter in milder climates, such as Southern California and the Gulf Coast. Ivy overwinters indoors in climates where winter temperatures dip below freezing. The ornamental cabbage lives out its brief annual life span in the container.

If you like, substitute a plant with a comparable, overall shape and size, such as an ornamental grass instead of the aster.

bowl of fire

right: **By planting mature specimens, you'll enjoy immediate gratification from this colorful garden. Smaller plants may take longer to bloom than mature plants, but they won't outgrow a pot as quickly.**

1 **organizing** Starting with mature blooming plants yields a more finished look that easily lasts a month or two. Blooming plants provide color without needing long-term fertilizing and grooming. A lightweight soilless potting mix works well, as long as it is consistently watered. Note the wide diameter of the pot used for this garden. It's large enough to accommodate six plants in close quarters.

2 **groundwork** First, place a small, square piece of window screen over the pot's drainage hole. This will keep out sowbugs and other pests as well as prevent soil from washing out of the hole. Pour in the soilless mix halfway up to the container's rim. Dampen the mix at this point or while it's still in the bag. Arrange the plants, still in their pots, into a portrait that looks balanced and shows off each plant to its best advantage.

3 **composing** Slip plants out of their pots and untangle the root balls. Set each plant firmly into its permanent place, spreading the root system over the soil. Pour in more mix until the roots are covered and the container is full. Tamp down the mix around the plants to anchor them securely. Water thoroughly. Lift the planted container to a wagon or wheeled plant caddy and roll it to its display location (either in full sun or partial shade).

portable color: tips

1   **root check** Root-bound plants have become dry and thirsty before you even bring them home. Once planted, they won't perform to potential. Avoid purchasing root-bound plant material; choose alternative plants. Inspect the drainage holes in larger potted plants for protruding roots, which indicate the plant has outgrown its pot. Slide smaller plants from their packs and check for tangled root balls.

As you plant container gardens, prime the plants' root systems for new growth by teasing or breaking open the root balls and spreading the roots out gently. Water potted plants before transplanting for easier removal from their original nursery containers. When starting with bare-root plants, keep them in a plastic bag and moisten regularly until planting.

2   **take a load off** Save on planting time, potting soil, and backaches with a few tricks tucked inside your chosen container. A small plastic nursery pot, inverted and propped on the bottom, takes up space that would otherwise be filled with soil, making the container easier to lift and carry. Fill the remainder of the pot with soil, leaving room for plants. Alternatively, recycle styrene packing material by using it as a filler for the bottom third of large containers. Also, use a decorative container, especially one without a drainage hole, as a cachepot for one or more plants in ordinary plastic nursery pots. The double layer insulates plants from heat and moisture evaporation.

change of seasons When the summer celebrities of your container garden fade at season's end, have some cool-season stand-ins ready. Fresh plant material keeps the garden's color going until frost. Mums, ornamental cabbages and kale, ornamental grasses, asters, fall crocus, pansies, dianthus, and snapdragons respond with vigor to the cool kiss of fall mornings. In the photo at left, asters, mums, and cape fuchsia take center stage for the fall color rally.

colorful colonies Container plants love company. Aesthetically, grouped containers have a much stronger impact than a lone potted plant. Garden designers recommend staging pots together in odd-number populations. Make one large container the focus of a potted garden, then encircle it with a supporting cast of smaller pots. A group of pots clustered together also creates a microclimate that protects the plant population from wind and heat. The shadows of surrounding pots shade root zones and keep them cool, promoting healthy growth during summer heat. Before you leave for vacation, crowd your containers together and water them thoroughly; they'll keep one another shaded and cool for several days.

For help visualizing what your garden might look like when you add elements, go to the interactive garden design tool at **www.bhg.com/bkplanagarden**

the
gardens

early-season gardens

spring portrait

Spring at first sight: a faint chartreuse haze veils the bare branches of winter. Suddenly, shooting stars and trilliums appear. The lawn hosts a brief showing of wild violets. Fruit tree blossoms paint the horizon with white clouds. Daffodil rivers run under trees. In California and the Southwest, flocks of poppies and lupines mark the end of the rainy season.

The palette expands by the week. Parades of lollipop-hue tulips march through gardens, and forsythias bear flowers of school-bus yellow. The soft pinks, whites, and lavenders of lilacs and peonies soon follow, trailing sweet perfumes.

Colors come and go quickly in this briefest of seasons, so plan for early-, mid-, and late-spring color. Wrap the brilliant blooms of bulbs in envelopes of flowering shrubs.

on the wall color

above: **Tulips are the undoubted stars in this rock wall scene, but more long-lasting color comes from pansies, candytuft, and gold-tint shrubs.**

post-chill thrills

opposite: **A welcome sight after a cold winter, forsythia and lively crowds of tulips require extended cold to bloom their best.**

great plants for early-season gardens

anemone	forsythia	peony
arabis	grape hyacinth	redbud
bleeding heart	hellebore	rhododendron
candytuft	iris	snowdrop
columbine	jack-in-the-pulpit	soapwort
crocus	lilac	trillium
cushion spurge	lily-of-the-valley	tulip
daffodil	lungwort	viola
dianthus	oriental poppy	wallflower
forget-me-not	pansy	white forsythia

midseason gardens

the curtain rises

Summer's first long days quicken the pace of plant growth and flowering. Traditional blooms, such as roses and delphiniums, begin unfurling to their season in the sun. Tropical cannas, callas, New Zealand flaxes, and fuchsias soar into action after the last frost date. Heat-worshipping annuals, including cosmos, zinnias, petunias, and sunflowers, keep company with perennial black-eyed Susans, lilies, coreopsis, and ornamental grasses.

The warm season brings its own challenge: How do you keep color waves breaking with no doldrums in between? Plan ahead.

cool summer shrine

right: 'Johnson's Blue' geranium, 'Elijah' blue fescue, 'Betty Prior' rose, and roly-poly alliums transform a plain urn and gray fountain into artwork. The soft color scheme also coordinates with the white house.

tropical fantasia

opposite: Romantic summer landscaping involves yellow canna, coneflowers, *Phygelius*, and New Zealand flax paired with the more traditional white lily and hydrangea.

great plants for midseason gardens

baby's breath	fuchsia
black-eyed susan	hydrangea
calendula	lavender
campanula	lily
canna	lobelia
cleome	ornamental grass
cosmos	rose
daylily	salvia
delphinium	veronica

midseason gardens

peak summer

Look to a succession of annuals in late spring and summer to fill gaps between perennials and to echo perennial color schemes.

Backdrops of single shrubs or trees that exhibit an interesting feature, such as colored foliage, berries, or textured bark, also anchor the summer garden while temporary color drifts arrive, and then melt away. Green shrubbery, such as herbs and boxwood, forms a frame that buffers bright, hot flower colors and knits the color scheme into an integrated vision.

Shape your summer border's core with perennials selected for spice whether in or out of bloom. Consider form and foliage beyond bloom color. Spiky perennials teamed up with mounded plants and gold leaves paired with multihue ones lend a sense of continuity during the season's hustle and bustle. Also, choose one dependable element, such as a hedge of ever-blooming roses or an herb-lined path in a linking color, and use it to join your garden's color blocks.

plant list

1 'six hills giant' catmint

2 borage

3 calendula

4 lavender

5 'the pearl' yarrow

6 dwarf boxwood

7 golden oregano

8 *iris pallida*

balancing act

left and *opposite:* The use of potted boxwoods, raised-bed frames, and architectural foliage (irises and alliums) introduces classical elements into a tousled flower and herb garden. Carefree perennials (catmint and yarrow) mingle with reseeding annuals (calendula and California poppies). In cold-winter climates, keep the potted boxwoods in a cool, sheltered place, such as a garage or sunporch, during the cold months.

garden color | **131**

late-season gardens

dazzling dog days

In late summer, heat-struck gardens often turn as sullen as the air just before a thunderstorm. Prevent garden color fatigue by planting long-blooming varieties. Use daylilies, such as 'Stella de Oro' or 'Bitsy', to brighten up a sunny border for several weeks.

Involve late-flowering perennials, including *Conoclinium coelestinum*, boltonia, aconite, Japanese anemone, and goldenrod, in your plan. They'll pick up color-theme threads where earlier-blooming perennials leave off. Plant several species within a plant group to enjoy a long-playing show. Asiatic, Oriental, and Regal (Trumpet) lilies provide varying bloom times and explosions of color.

bright lights

above right: **'Enchantment' Asiatic lilies, baby's breath, Shasta daisies, and 'Bonica' roses offer a rare late-summer freshness.**

lily allure

right: **Fragrant *Lilium regale* and daylilies have late- and long-blooming tendencies.**

late show

opposite: **A late-season flowering paradise is possible in this Zone 5 garden because it includes marathon bloomers and late varieties.**

late-season gardens

ripened color

Late-season gardens offer a perfect opportunity to show off plants in their second prime. Many annuals and perennials have richly colored and textured ornamental seedpods. Pearly disks of lunaria flutter in the breeze. Cardoon and teasel seed heads resemble intricately woven baskets. Allium flower heads imitate miniature satellites.

Rose species that develop large hips will start doing so now if faded blooms aren't removed. Viburnum, pyracantha, hawthorn, and dogwood become laden with berries. Besides the rich patina they add to garden palettes, plants allowed to go to seed also make your yard a destination favored by wildlife, especially migratory birds.

great plants for late-season gardens

amaranth	goldenrod
astilbe (late-blooming)	japanese anemone
baby's breath	joe-pye weed
celosia	lunaria
coreopsis 'moonbeam'	mistflower
daylily 'stella de oro'	regal lily
delphinium	rose
echinacea	salvia
feverfew	shasta daisy

go wild

right: Fall migratory birds will flock to this free-for-all corner of a harvest garden. The colorful smorgasbord of sunflower, goldenrod, *Lunaria*, amaranth, and coneflower pleases the eye and bird palates too.

A few perennials rebloom as days grow shorter, after first flowering in early summer. Some bearded iris varieties, delphinium, and clematis share this remontant (reblooming) timing. Additional perennials prolong their colorful performance if sheared back after a midsummer flowering. This list includes black-eyed Susan, coreopsis, and helenium. Chrysanthemums produce large late-season flowers if buds are removed until midsummer.

With minimal nurturing and maximum planning, the summer garden sustains the show through its very last curtain call. A top layer of compost applied in fall and spring, plus a sprinkling of slow-release fertilizer or organic nutrients early in the season, ensures that summer's promise comes true.

big picture
above left: **Layers of ornamental grasses, dahlias, and chrysanthemums compose a blazing fall scenario. Dig dahlias' tuberous roots and store them indoors over winter in cold climates.**

summer meets fall
left: **Tender Mexican sage *(Salvia leucantha)*, lamb's-ears, and a flurry of white Japanese anemone flowers stand up to the brilliant fall colors of chrysanthemums.**

garden color | **135**

harvest-season gardens

gilded fall gardens

In fall, more so than any other season, brilliant pigments come from sources other than flowers. Changing foliage of trees and shrubs, ripened seed heads, and bronzed ornamental grasses all share in creating the richest of the seasonal palettes.

Ornamental grasses endow the autumnal garden with a slightly untamed look. Imposing and rhythmic in the wind, they deepen dramatically in color as temperatures drop and days shorten. Combined with perennials that bloom late, including *Rudbeckia*, *Sedum spectabile*, Russian sage, aster, and mum, grasses add delicate texture to the fall garden. They project a sense of haunting wistfulness at the blooming season's end. Their show will go on, however, extending architecture and rare color into the winter garden. For that reason, as well as the cover and seeds they offer wildlife, delay trimming grasses until early spring.

autumn rainbows

above right: **There's plenty of flower power left in this fall border of** *Polygonum* **'Firetail',** *Echinacea* **'White Swan', astilbe, and shrubby** *Caryopteris*. **These perennials will continue to provide food and shelter for overwintering wildlife, so spring is the best time to prune.**

roadside attractions

right: **A brilliant-color cornucopia of fall blooms, including aster, dahlia, sunflower, ornamental oregano, and lamb's-ear, attracts human and winged visitors for exploration.**

enter fall

opposite: **A magnificent, undisciplined planting mixes late-blooming perennials such as globe thistle, coneflower, butterfly bush, and ornamental grasses with sweet potato vine. The warm fall color scheme reflects the home's facade.**

harvest-season gardens

reaping riches

Fall glory realizes the best-laid plans made in spring. Trees and shrubs planted then pay dividends in spectacular fall foliage. Oaks, birches, beeches, dogwoods, maples (Japanese maples, in particular), ginkgos, persimmons, and sweet gums show their autumnal colors with the cooler weather.

Many perennials also show reddened or gilded leaves at the first touch of frost. Those with changing fall color include epimedium, peony, gaura, *Geranium psilostemon*, and some euphorbias. Shrubs such as euonymus, oakleaf hydrangea, aronia, sumac, viburnum, and blueberry also catch fire in the fall, as do grapes, Virginia creeper, Boston ivy, and other vines.

The blooming continues in the autumn garden as dahlia, Joe-pye weed, mistflower (*Conoclinium*

autumn jewels

above right: **The fiery plumes of late-flowering annual celosia pair with perennial *Rudbeckia*, milkweed, ornamental grass, fern, and thinleaf zinnia. It's a border scheme that birds will seek out for seeds.**

metallic magic

right: **Japanese maples flame with fall color. Perennial *Epimedium*, *Rodgersia*, fern, and hellebore skirt the maples with copper, bronze, and scarlet.**

coelestinum), milkweed, and aconite display their finest flower color. Many blooms attract butterflies in their fall migration. Autumn-flowering clematis (*C. ternifolia* 'Sweet Autumn') wafts a sweet scent and enhances fall's textural collage with its fluffy seed heads. Warm-weather annuals, including zinnia, celosia, globe amaranth, and castor bean, continue blooming vigorously until the first frost. Gardeners in warm regions can also find unusual sources of fall color in the bronze and purple leaves of tropical cannas and bananas, plus a variety of brilliant-color houseplants.

Harvest now to bring the garden's color indoors with arrangements of dried flowers and seed heads. Also collect ripened seeds to regenerate your garden "paints" for the next year's palette.

great plants for harvest-season gardens

aster	milkweed
black-eyed susan	mistflower
broom corn	ornamental grasses
canna	ornamental kale
chrysanthemum	pansy
clematis ternifolia	russian sage
globe thistle	sedum 'autumn joy'
japanese maple	spicebush
knot weed	sumac

brazen duo
left: **Who would have thought that North American native Joe-pye weed and tropical bronze-leaf canna would hit it off so well? Both tall plants benefit from moist soil. Store tender canna roots indoors over the winter.**

multiseason garden

altered states

The same garden wears three different costumes that change with the season. Spring's color plan shifts easily into summer's with no lag if executed by planning ahead.

Hardy annuals such as godetia, dianthus, candytuft, stock, sweet alyssum, and pansy go into the ground before spring's last frost, which they can survive. Their color progresses into early summer. Meanwhile, more tender summer annuals get an inconspicuous green start, hidden behind the spring blooms.

As summer blooms wane and mums replace them, ornamental grasses and asters come to the fore, dominating the landscape with broad sweeps of texture.

spring pink
above right: **The cottage gets a lift from a pink-theme tulip bed rimmed in grape hyacinths.**

summer yellow
right: **Snapdragons and marigolds replace tulips, filling in among perennial *Rudbeckias*.**

fall gold
opposite: **Maiden grass and fountain grass round out the fall palette, along with lavender aster and bronze mum.**

multiseason garden

color transition tips

Spend the bulk of your color budget on prominent areas. Keep the color fresh and ever changing in those places, such as the front door or along a well-trod path. Focus on generous plantings around hardscape features, including rock outcroppings, arbors, walkways, fountains, and other destinations where people will enter or linger awhile.

Make seasonal transitions colorful and effortless with these strategies: Start planning for the next

transient spring

right: **Spring bulbs, including grape hyacinths, anemones, and tulips, pop up amid hardy annuals planted early in the season. 'Goldflame' spirea across the bridge and newly emerged sedum provide perennial landmarks.**

great plants for multiseason gardens

early-season	coneflower
anemone	delphinium
candytuft	impatiens
creeping phlox	scabiosa
grape hyacinth	twinspur
hellebore	veronica
silene	**late-season**
spirea 'goldflame'	aster
sweet pea	black-eyed susan
tulip	chrysanthemum
vinca	marigold
midseason	sedum
bergenia	toad lily
chamomile	verbena

season before it starts. Create space by removing whatever's tired or underperforming. Treat spring tulips as annuals, planting them thickly the previous fall, then lifting them before the foliage fades. Dig up faded summer annuals and plug in mums at summer's end.

Refresh summer borders by pruning and roguing tired plants. Keep an out-of-the-way nursery bed planted with leftover pack plants, immature perennials, or extra annuals you've started from seed. These will supply your borders with fresh-face reinforcements as summer marches on. Overwinter any leftover perennials in the nursery and transplant them into the garden the following year.

Pack window boxes and other containers densely with plants big enough for instant impact. As portable gardens, potted plants earn their keep in high-exposure areas.

When planting late-season borders, select quart- or gallon-size perennials. The plants flower the first year and grow large enough to divide their second season, thus returning your initial investment. Ornamental grasses also represent money well spent, because they make colorful contributions in three seasons, not just one. Plant bulbs in fall plus early annuals in spring to camouflage stubs of trimmed grasses.

short summer
above left: **A footbridge with a rock garden in the foreground serves as a focal point year-round. Salmon impatiens, blue veronica, and 'Lulu' marigold brighten the edges.**

extended fall
left: **Perennial sedums and sedges, combined with freshly planted mums, adorn the bridge garden with fall highlights. The mums fill gaps left behind by spent summer annuals.**

extending color

shortcuts to success

Propagating plants by division gives your garden broad brushstrokes of color in a short time. Once mature, perennial plants yield several divisions, allowing you to repeat the color groupings throughout your borders. Take the fastest route by starting your garden with larger plants in one-gallon pots. They'll be ready to divide within a year or two.

Divide root balls of perennials either in spring or fall, depending on plant bloom times. Large-leaf, unwieldy plants, such as hostas, ornamental grasses, and daylilies, divide more easily if dug in early spring when the plants emerge. Divide and replant lilies-of-the-valley, Shasta daisies, hellebores, astilbes, and other early-spring-flowering perennials in fall.

multiplied by root division

astilbe	oregano
coreopsis	ornamental grasses
daylily	peony
ferns	phlox
gaura	salvia
hellebore	sedum
hosta	shasta daisy
iris	thyme
lily-of-the-valley	vinca

divide to multiply

right: 'Moonbeam' coreopsis, 'Elijah' blue fescue, 'Autumn Joy' sedum, lavender, purple coneflower, and Russian sage are just a few of the many perennials that respond well to root division.

1 dig In fall, trim back a perennial before dividing the plant. (Less bulk on top makes divisions easier to pull apart.) Then insert a sharp-edge spade or pitchfork and dig around the plant's circumference. Dig around the plant again to completely dislodge it. Use the spade or fork under the plant to help lift it. Plants lift more easily in dry weather when you water them thoroughly the day you plan to divide them.

2 lift out Lift the plant, including the root ball and attached soil, from the garden. If the plant doesn't move easily, reinsert the shovel to detach any clinging roots. Squat and use your leg muscles to lift the plant and avoid back injury. Place the plant on nearby ground. Trim back the tops of thickly thatched perennials such as ornamental grasses, bamboos, and coreopsis. It will make the dividing easier to accomplish.

3 divide Although this process is called root division, it actually separates parts of the plant crown with roots attached. Use your hands to push the plant stems to either side, locating a natural part in the crown. Then use a sharp-edge spade to divide the plant in half. Divide the halves into additional sections, if you like. Replant the divisions and water thoroughly.

changeable hydrangeas

A constant source of summer garden color comes
from the billowy blooms of hydrangeas. Stalwart
shrubs for shade, they live for years and display
handsome foliage when their bloom period is past.
Several hydrangea hybrids, plus a handful of
species, are available by mail order, or check with
your local garden center's shrub department. Plant
a variety of hydrangeas to have color waves
from early summer to fall and fresh or dried
flowers indoors.

Many varieties of *Hydrangea macrophylla* (bigleaf
or mophead and lacecap) respond to soil pH. In
acidic soil, plants produce spectacular blue blooms.
Alkaline to neutral soils yield rosy pink flowers
that age to magenta. Treat garden soil to alter
bloom color by adding iron sulfate or elemental
sulfur to acidify or hydrated lime or superphosphate
to boost alkalinity. Two basics to remember: Know
your soil's pH before you start and apply soil
amendments before flower buds appear. It may
take several months for a color change to develop.
Some white-flowering types and some new varieties
retain their color regardless of the soil pH.

Crisp white blooms of the peegee hydrangea
and towering snow cones of oakleaf hydrangea
offer summer refreshment too, especially in
partially shaded sites. A color bonus: the foliage
of these species reddens in fall.

flaunt those big blues

right: Cool lavender-blue mophead hydrangeas
create a welcoming oasis for relaxing in the
garden. A naturally acidic soil enhances the
color. Boost soil acidity by adding iron sulfate
or elemental sulfur (¼ cup dissolved in a gallon
of water).

hydrangea alchemy
left: Some pink hydrangea varieties shift color from green to cream, deepen to pink, and then age to magenta. To help cut hydrangeas stay fresh longer, crush stem ends with a hammer before placing them in water.

lasting pleasure
below: Harvest hydrangea blooms in late summer or early fall and dry them for months of enjoyment indoors. Let flowers air dry in a vase without water.

garden color | **147**

extending color

comeback color

Timely plant manicures thwart plants' natural goal of seed setting, thus guaranteeing a continuous supply of flower color. Any plant that belongs to the composite or daisy family, especially, benefits from occasional flower snipping. This includes zinnia, coreopsis, aster, boltonia, marguerite, helenium, and other summer garden stars.

Stimulate bloom by feeding perennials with a low-nitrogen, high-phosphorus fertilizer (5-10-5); give annuals a balanced (10-10-10) formula.

snip and grow

right: Dense-flowering zinnias run a constant race toward seed setting to ensure future generations. The more faded flower heads are removed, the more new blooms form.

rose grooming

below: Long-blooming roses, such as 'Sally Holmes' and 'Joseph's Coat', continue their color show all summer. Stimulate flowering by cutting just-open blooms for vase life or snipping spent blooms.

mulch A coat of insulating mulch 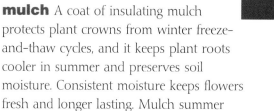 protects plant crowns from winter freeze-and-thaw cycles, and it keeps plant roots cooler in summer and preserves soil moisture. Consistent moisture keeps flowers fresh and longer lasting. Mulch summer flower borders and shrubs with 1 to 2 inches of organic material, including chopped leaves, shredded bark, cocoa bean hulls, or compost.

snap off Showcase daylily flowers and other plants that develop several blooms per stalk in a manner they deserve by snapping off blooms past their prime. Lilies, gladiolas, crocosmias, hollyhocks, and irises all benefit from this action. Pull down gently on the withered flower until it snaps off cleanly.

snip Signal the next wave of blooms to form by clipping off stems of withered flowers. Snipping rejuvenates all types of flowers that grow in spikes, such as delphinium, veronica, salvia, and foxglove, as well as yarrow, rose, and daisy types. Use hand pruners or sharp scissors to deadhead flowers on fibrous stems. Cut off the faded flowers about ¼ inch above the next bud. Snipping encourages new blooms on coneflowers, coreopsis, hostas, and zinnias.

pinch Crops of maximum-size flowers reward the gardener who disbuds plants such as mums, dahlias, carnations, and peonies. Disbudding diverts the flow of growth hormones, food, and water from many to a few stems and remaining buds. Pinch off all but the main bud on a stem.

lasting color

lingering looks

The longest-lasting color comes from permanent garden features. When researching garden candidates, keep your region's climate in mind. Plants that melt with mildew won't endure hot and humid Southeast summers. Mountain gardeners want annuals that tolerate warm days and cool nights with equal aplomb, getting off to a fast start equal to the short growing season. Southwest gardeners need plants that flourish in dry summers. Plants native to your region or to similar climates have the best potential. Search out hybrids developed from these well-adapted plants.

top 10 perennials for lasting color

baby's breath	gaillardia
campanula (dwarf)	scabiosa
coreopsis	valerian
cranesbill	veronica
evening primrose	yarrow

don juan and friends
above right: Ordinary lattice becomes a wall of color when it supports a long-blooming 'Don Juan' rose. Tender tropicals, including coleus, impatiens, and ornamental sweet potato vine, bask in the shade of the rosy canopy.

annual showstopper
right: 'Mr. Wonderful' coleus dazzles all season without fuss.

spicy border
opposite: Orange marigolds and variegated sage punch up the color quotient in a garden where bright pots provide portable color.

lasting color

marathon blooms

Color plays a significant role in flower breeding. Because fashion and decorating color trends shift so rapidly, however, seed companies focus more on long-range patterns, including consumer interest in unusual flower colors and variegated leaves.

Breeders also select flowers with long-lasting colors. Among pansies, a blue-flowering variety usually opens first and lasts longest, possibly because its wild viola ancestors all originally had blue flowers. Yellow, orange, and red flowers hold up best when exposed to strong sun, so these shades receive attention in new bedding plant varieties, especially for hotter climates. Early bloomers get special focus from bedding plant breeders because of an emphasis on pack plants that will show strong color while sitting on garden-center shelves.

cascading color
right: **Nierembergia, heliotrope, and golden dahlberg daisy keep the color waves rolling when faded flowers are sheared off. Pools of silver artemisia enhance the hot colors.**

cool corner
below: **Lobelia and pansy flowers glow against concrete edging. Deadheading flowers prompts rebloom.**

lissie who?

left: In the wild, the satiny flowers and blue-gray leaves of lisianthus have evolved to deflect heat and survive hot, arid conditions. Flower breeders have developed hybrids for long-lived cut flowers and drought-tolerant bedding plants.

summer parasols

below: Cosmos produce multitudes of silky petals in pink, magenta, white, yellow, and orange. This summer annual grows from scattered seed. Clip off spent flowers weekly. Harvest seeds at the season's end for next year.

top 10 annuals for lasting color

cleome	marigold
cosmos	nasturtium
geranium	nierembergia
impatiens	portulaca
lisianthus	sweet pea

lasting color

hardy breeds

Certain flowers come with a long-term color warranty. Their durability relates to petal thickness and how tightly the blossoms hold to the plant, as well as the plant's relative hardiness.

Perennials that flower the longest include blue flax, catmint (*Nepeta*), campanula, aster, scabiosa, veronica, spiderwort, fringed bleeding heart, evening primrose, and phlox. It's no accident of breeding that most of these are native North American plants. For an extensive list of plants searchable by name, type, and even bloom color, go to **www.bhg.com/bkplantindex**

Not all garden color trends prove lasting. That collection of green flowers you had to have last year may not suit your fancy next year. Keep in mind that your garden evolves with your tastes, so go ahead and plant a bed of your current favorite flowers and enjoy.

prairie palette

above right: **Perennial coneflowers and black-eyed Susans hail from the prairie, where their flowers cheerfully endure intense heat.**

sunny spotlight

right: **A concrete birdbath becomes the center of attention when surrounded by flattering hues of 'Early Sunrise' coreopsis, 'Heritage' rose, *Campanula carpatica*, 'Goldflame' spirea, and spiderwort.**

hummer haven

left: Bee balm, annual red salvia, nicotiana, and 'Blue Butterfly' dwarf delphinium attract hummingbirds. Many flowers with prolonged color supply nectar for hummers throughout the summer.

hot and hotter

below: Two perennials prized for long-lasting blooms, coreopsis and daylily, warm summer borders with an array of sizzling golds, oranges, and reds. Snap off faded daylily blooms to encourage healthy plants. Deadhead coreopsis and a wave of new blooms will appear.

artists' gardens: oregon

This Pacific Northwest watercolorist tints her one-acre masterpiece in Portland with the same vibrant hues as her paintings. Each of the garden's six rooms reflects her talent for harmonizing plant textures and hardscape elements. Pottery, stone benches, and paving work cohesively with color themes. Half the garden is shady, so the garden artist plants layers of intriguing foliage in textural contrasts. Sun lovers, including her favorite daylily, take center stage in the exposed front-yard border. Flowering shrubs complete the plant palette.

chris keylock williams

In gardening, as well as in art, patience and the creative process bring unexpected results. "The things that go wrong lead me to try something new that turns out to be even more successful than I had hoped. I paint a background a different color and the flowers suddenly pop out. That happens in the garden too. I struggle with certain plants and have to give up and go on to some other idea. I let the design evolve."

Clockwise, from left:

mellow ambience
Gold-and-green
variegated holly provides
a flattering backdrop for
the yellow *Brugmansia*
in a rustic urn. The
overall effect is protected
and intimate.

light and dark
A crazy quilt of textures
makes this shady bed pop
visually. Starry-flower
campanula, hydrangea,
hosta, Australian violet,
and a seasonal focus of
impatiens mix it up under
a flowering plum tree.

sun catchers
A sunny border of daylily
celebrities shines brighter
when complemented with
the gray lace foliage and
gold button blooms of
curry plant. 'Helaman',
an orange-rim daylily,
stands in the foreground.
A fawn-color flagstone
path meandering through
the borders harmonizes
with the warm-color
flower palette.

lessons from the gardener

- Bright-hue daylilies look more color saturated when combined with silvery foliage, including curry plant and artemisia, or fine-texture plants such as feverfew.
- Compose garden scenes by highlighting flowers and foliage with objects, such as pottery, a bench, or a birdbath.
- Where shade prevails, contrast broad sweeps of dark and light colors in your garden paintings.
- Juxtapose prominent hosta foliage with the delicate blades of gold or lime green carex grass. Carex, or sedge, enjoys the same moist conditions as hostas.

artists' gardens: iowa

The rolling rural landscape boasts a gem of a garden that includes only the hardiest plants. Its artist specializes in composing vignettes that bring out the colorful personalities of perennials. All can stand up to the rigors of Midwest weather with minimal tending. The garden's island beds spill over with free-form portraits of perennials displaying their best potential.

karen strohbeen

The first priority in the art of combining perennials: "Mostly you should please yourself," says Karen. To compose a botanical painting, she suggests a stroll through your yard to gather materials. Place flowers and foliage in a vase and arrange them into a portrait you find attractive. That's how to approach garden designing, as well. Be open to possibilities; take chances, Karen advises. Plant some personality or whimsy in your garden.

lessons from the gardener

- Use gray foliage as a color enhancer, especially with pastel colors. Any flower color looks stronger when standing next to gray.
- Plant densely in superb soil that is well amended with compost and peat moss. Set plants roughly 25 percent closer than their labels suggest. This creates a living mulch that crowds out weeds and reduces maintenance.
- Train a clematis to climb through an evergreen by planting the vine about a foot away from the tree trunk and gently tying it to the boughs until the vine wends its own way.

Clockwise, from top left:

connecting dots

A 'Betty Prior' rose shines against the fuzzy texture of a dwarf baby's breath (*Gypsophila paniculata* 'Compacta') and blue *Allium caeruleum*.

nurture nature

Karen starts new plants in nursery beds and learns about their growth habits, bloom time, compatibility, and disease problems before moving them into the garden.

carefree combo

Blue *Clematis × durandii* contrasts in color and shape with the flat flower heads of golden 'Moonshine' yarrow and dots of *Allium caeruleum*.

spring sunrise

Newly emerged mounds of green-and-gold perennial foliage highlight the variegated leaves of *Iris pallida* 'Aureo-variegata' and the blue spikes of grape hyacinth.

peaks and valleys

A purple tower of *Clematis × jackmanii* accents a bed of 'Bitsy' daylily, *Iris spuria*, and golden barberry. Dwarf evergreen trees round out the scene.

This urban living art gallery was planted with a

jackhammer. An asphalt driveway has given way to drifts of flower and leaf artistry that reflect the region's constantly changing light. Within sedate arborvitae walls, the plantings showcase a richly painted house in a nine-color coat of terra-cotta to teal. Bowling balls, urns, and other art pieces punctuate the rippling curves of borders and an extensive container garden. Art takes shape everywhere, with a sense of humor and fun.

lessons from the gardener

- Direct the eye within your garden compositions: Echo the same plant repeatedly in a diagonal pattern.
- Instead of planting solid blocks of color, take a more subtle, naturalistic approach. Repeat a plant farther back in the border to create a sense of depth and a self-sown look.
- Artful elements such as colorful bowling balls and vintage chairs, when well placed, fuse garden beds into exuberant configurations.
- When trees and shrubs reach full leaf during the growing season, mark where you plan to create arches and openings with late-winter pruning.

Clockwise, from top left:

gallery showing

A potted garden gathers around an artful table and a bowling ball. *Clematis × jackmanii* sprawls out to form a purple backdrop.

bowling ball chic

A bowling ball poised in an Art Deco stand echoes the coppery color of bladder senna, or *Colutea*, flowers dangling from above.

electric eclectic

Potted salvia, New Zealand flax, and assorted succulents set off the painted terra-cotta and teal house exterior. These plants thrive in the hot, dry conditions created by sun reflecting off concrete.

valerie murray

The art of gardening entails relating smaller groups to the larger overall picture through echoes and transitions, says Valerie. But a garden is not like a painting that "needs to be hung and demands to be looked at. You can't hang onto it, you have to be in the moment. It is about process, like music, and when the light changes, everything changes."

artists' gardens: missouri

On the edge of the woods and prairie, the possibilities of single colors play out when massed in individual beds. The paintbox garden encircles a stucco garden shed centerpiece. Each corner of the romantic spread curves into transitional areas that lead to an orchard, a vegetable garden, an arbor, and a woodland border. Enriched soil keeps the color flowing.

ouida touchón

"Monet liked masses of color, and he painted the garden with blooming plants. I attempt to do the same thing in a much smaller space ... . I think of garden design as an art form. When I'm planting, I am considering color and bloom time, but I'm also considering the way the forms of one plant will work with the forms and shapes of the other plants. I look at it in a three-dimensional way."

Clockwise, from opposite top:

spring things

In Ouida's pink garden, 'Imperial Pink' pansies contribute a whole spectrum of watercolor-tinted petals, from rosy to deep plum, through the spring. She snaps off faded flowers to prolong the annual pansy's life in the garden and continue its color parade.

garden blues

Ouida holds a watercolor inspired by her blue garden, which is visible in the background.

beyond greens

The bronze and deep green of 'Rouge d'Hiver' lettuce leaves sparkle in the sun and capture the artistic gardener's attention. Lettuce makes a brilliant edging plant for flower beds as well as vegetable plots.

room with a view

A stucco garden shed (not shown) overlooks the blue garden, where ageratum, globe thistle, salvia, butterfly bush, and forget-me-not share their misty blue hues among drifts of silvery lamb's-ears and dusty miller. *Tuteurs* in the far corners support roses, while an urn captivates from the center of the formal design.

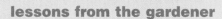

lessons from the gardener

- A formal design, featuring a series of separate beds, facilitates organization of plantings devoted to single colors, such as yellow, orange, red, pink, purple, and blue.
- Weave potted annuals into a perennial border to provide substitute color during lapses in blooms.
- Develop transitional areas, including curved paths and arbors, to link formal and casual garden plantings.
- A repetitive edging, such as dianthus or santolina, gives the most eclectic or sprawling garden a cohesive look.
- Possibilities for a blue garden include ageratum, globe thistle, 'Sky Beauty' Dutch iris, 'Victoria' salvia, anchusa, brunnera, butterfly bush, allium, sea holly, borage, blue lobelia, and forget-me-not.

california

A floating feather, a tiny cucumber, jewel-like berries, and other garden minutiae fuel this artist's imagination. On a tree-sheltered hillside above the sea, the garden has a natural beauty that prompts sketches of bugs and blossoms. Well-nurtured vegetable and cutting plots flourish. Rugged, time-tested plants survive grazing deer. Birds find a paradise of food and shelter here.

lessons from the gardener

- Plant bearded iris, crocosmia, camellias, rhododendrons, Texas privet, and herbs, such as lavender and lemon balm, for hardy color additions that won't tempt deer.
- Provide water in protected spaces to entice birds into the garden.
- Old broken-down ladders have a second life in the garden as props for fast-growing vines.
- Interplant flowers, herbs, fruits, and vegetables for a richly diverse garden.
- Organically grown vegetable gardens produce high yields using the intensive method: deeply dug soil enriched with compost and leaf mold, carefully spaced plantings, and raised beds.

maryjo koch

Gardeners experience an intimacy with nature every day, Maryjo observes. They become artists of sorts the minute their hands touch soil. "When you're gardening, you're really observing and getting into it, just like when you're painting. You're touching the soil and feeling the soil and getting your hands into it. You're distinguishing certain smells: The smells of the soil, the smell after it rains, the fragrance of all the flowers. Those details become a part of you, just as when you paint."

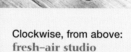

Clockwise, from above:
fresh–air studio
A weathered bench, warmed by the sun and flanked by pots of foliage plants, becomes the best seat in the house for capturing the garden's ongoing drama on paper.

natural studies
Today's garden stars become future art. Just-picked dwarf sunflowers pose in a vase. A potting bench doubles as an outdoor painting table.

careful observation
The crinkled leaves and delicate blossoms of scented geraniums delight the nose with their crisp fragrances and entice the eye with their textures. These frost-tender plants must come inside for the winter everywhere except along the mild-winter West Coast.

color
decor

structures

the bigger picture

Garden structures
play a major role as
ambassadors of color.
They carry your chosen
palette throughout the
landscape in ways that
plants can't. A vividly
painted arbor or trellis
fills in the gaps at
times when plant color
has ebbed.

The first structure to
consider? Your house.
In fact, take a long
look at your house's
exterior before planting
anything in the ground.
You may hesitate to
paint the entire house
in your favorite hues,
but consider shutters
and the front door
as the threshold of
color possibilities.

open-and-shut color
right: **Blue shutters or
a blue garden bench
alone might not have
been sufficient to
make this shady
garden stand out.
Repeating the color
theme on both levels
has more impact,
especially when paired
with pink blooms.**

blue times two

left: In this narrow passage, the yellow gate stands in for flowers. Not visible is the garden beyond, liberally dotted with yellow blooms.

arizona zeal

below left: Outdoor fabric and painted concrete echo the intense blue of the desert sky.

shed chic

below right: The earthy tones of exterior stain turn an ordinary bench and shed into a magnetic setting.

furnishings

color feasts

Garden furniture gives you a vantage point for appreciating your finished garden painting. It also intensifies and completes the palette you begin with plants. A brilliant color, such as red or orange, becomes a full-fledged garden scheme when flowers have the companionship of a chair or a bench in the same hue.

Choices abound in garden styles of seating as well as materials and finishes. The style should take its cue from both house architecture and the feel of the garden. Among materials, choose cedar or teak for longevity and year-round outdoor endurance. If you plan to paint bare wood, then select cedar or pine. Plastic or resin chairs offer an economical, easy-to-wash alternative in garden furniture. Wicker looks natural, blends with most flower colors, and endows gardens with a classic casual look. For durability and a more formal fit, invest in metal furniture. Old metal or old wicker can be repainted with your favorite bright colors.

A seat flanked with colorfully planted pots creates focus in a small garden or a cozy corner in a large space. Place seating areas where they're shaded at least part of the day but with a full garden view. Add interest to a shady place with a chair or a bench painted in a luminous color.

take a seat

To tie a garden seat into background plantings, choose a similar color or complement. Old-fashioned Adirondack chairs offer timeless appeal with their casual comfort and easy-to-paint construction. *Clockwise from opposite top:* Green-painted ladderback chairs and a blue tablecloth contribute to a relaxing dining spot on an enclosed patio. A rosy pink makes surrounding flowers pop out of the shade. A bench cushion reflects the soft pastels of surrounding flowers. Blue-painted Adirondack chairs coordinate with gray flagstone and gravel, taking the color scheme a bolder step forward. A sunflower-color chair with a floral print cushion works with the plant scheme. A red chair makes the shade hum with color and looks crisp with the Shasta daisies.

a garden house

zones	make it	skill
all	1 month	advanced

you will need

- shovel
- concrete premix
- concrete blocks
- anchor bolts
- 2×4s, 1×6s
- salvaged windows
- salvaged door
- plexiglass
- clear vinyl tarp
- wood siding
- architectural details (optional)
- exterior–grade paint or stain

plant playhouse

Hatch your garden's color scheme in a cozy greenhouse that requires minimal woodworking skills. The fairytale charm of this building (*right*) derives from the doors and windows gathered from thrift shops and neighbors' throwaways.

Erect your garden house on a concrete foundation. Excavate, then use concrete blocks to frame the foundation. Fill and cover the blocks with concrete. While the concrete is wet, insert anchor bolts and leave half of each protruding above the concrete surface. Allow several days for the concrete to cure. Drying time depends on the weather.

Construct the house's framework in sections to accommodate the windows, door, walls, and roof. Use a plexiglass roof that withstands wind and hail better than glass but admits light just as well. Make the edges leakproof by fastening a clear vinyl tarp over the roof. Build benches along the interior walls of the shed to hold potted plants and seedling trays, if you like. Leave the dirt floor bare, or cover it with a few inches of pea gravel.

garden hideaway

right: **A focal point in a shady backyard, this 5×9-foot greenhouse wears shades of serene green and periwinkle blue.**

1 frame Build a series of four 2×4 frames to accommodate the windows and door in your greenhouse plan. Join the house frames together to form walls, fastening them to the anchor bolts protruding from the concrete foundation. Attach the roof rafters, made of 2×4s, to the tops of the walls. The roof shown is steeply pitched to fit a special stained-glass window at one end. You may want a flatter roof.

2 windows and doors Nail 1×6s horizontally across the roof rafters to steady the rafters in place and serve as nailers for the plexiglass covering. Nail 2×4s upright in the front and back walls to stabilize the roof. Install windows in the wall frames. Install a door in one wall. You may need to trim the door to fit the opening. Nail wood siding to the outside walls. Add architectural trim or other details, if you like. Finish the house, using exterior-grade paint or stain.

3 special features Include a stained-glass window or pieces of decorative tile as a personal touch in your garden house design. Fit custom-cut glass around the window or tiles. Other options include a birdhouse, an old clock, a thermometer, or other found art. A practical design could include a window or a vent that opens and closes to help regulate the temperature and humidity in the house.

a vine pole

zones	make it	skill
all	2 hours	moderate

you will need

- two 8-foot-long 2×4s
- one 4-foot-long 1×4
- exterior-grade wood glue
- one 3-foot-long 1×6
- two 4-foot ¾-inch-diameter dowels cut into 6-inch pieces
- one 3½-inch (approx.) wood finial with dowel bolt
- four 3-inch-long galvanized deck screws
- exterior stain or sealer; or primer and paint

going up!

This 6-foot-tall structure gives your color garden an aerial accent. Plant it to prop annual vines, such as black-eyed Susan, morning glory, or sweet pea, or a perennial clematis, hardy kiwi, or climbing rose.

Cut 12 square spacers (4×4-inch) from 1×4 treated lumber. Starting at the top, locating the first spacer flush with the top ends of the 2×4s, glue the spacers (3½ inches apart) between a pair of treated 2×4s. Use exterior-grade wood glue and bond the spacers to the 2×4s; clamp them until the glue dries.

morning glory

right and *below:* **Give your flower garden a colorful lift with a pegged pole that supports vines, such as morning glories. Top the pole with a small birdhouse or a weather vane instead of a finial.**

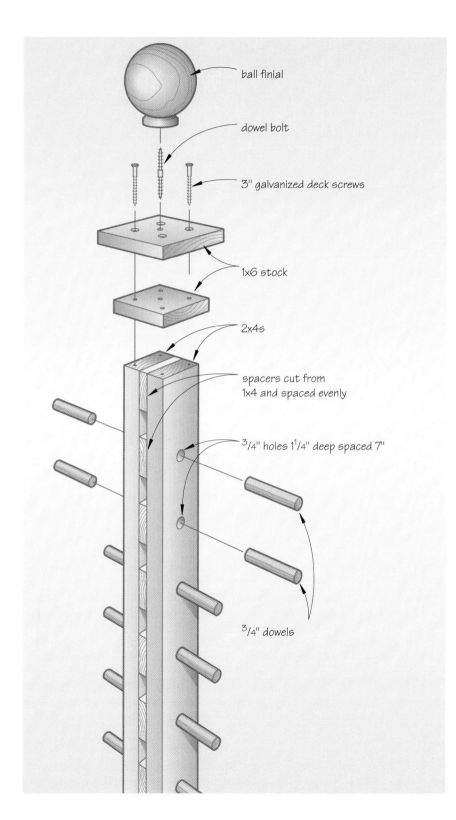

ball finial

dowel bolt

3" galvanized deck screws

1x6 stock

2x4s

spacers cut from
1x4 and spaced evenly

$^3/4$" holes $1^1/4$" deep spaced 7"

$^3/4$" dowels

aim high

above: Use cedar or pressure-treated lumber;
build two poles to create symmetrical shapes
at a garden entrance.

Drill holes in the pole sides for the 6-inch
dowels and glue them in place. Cut the squares for
the top, as shown, from the 1×6 and screw them
into position using deck screws.

Fasten the ball finial to the top with a dowel
bolt (a specialty fastener that has screw threads
on both ends). Drill a pilot hole, and then twist the
bolt into the hole by gripping the center of it with
locking pliers.

Finish the wood with exterior stain or sealer;
or prime and paint it.

Set the pole in the ground at least 24 inches
deep to stabilize it.

garden color | **175**

a trellis trio

zones	make it	skill
all	1 day	moderate

you will need

- eight 8-foot-long 2×4s
- sixteen 8-foot-long 1×2s
- one 6-foot-long 2×10
- power miter saw
- 1¼-inch 3d galvanized nails
- deck screws
- exterior-grade wood glue
- 3-inch galvanized deck screws
- saber saw
- crushed rock
- exterior stain or sealer; or primer and paint

garden dividers

Every room should have a versatile piece of furniture that accomplishes many functions. This trellis trio performs the same feat in a garden room. Not only do they support vines, but when stood together, the structures form a corner screen. Placed side by side, this trellis trio creates a privacy fence beautifully cloaked in vines or climbing roses.

Begin building them by taking six of the eight 2×4 posts and cutting a 30-degree angle at the top end, using a power miter saw for best results. Cut the 1×2 brackets and center each side-to-side inside a post, with the top end 1½ inches from the angled cut on the post. Nail the brackets in place.

To make the lattice part of the trellis, first create points at the tops of the nine 1×2 uprights by cutting two 45-degree angles; then cut the uprights to the right length. Cut the 1×2 trellis rails, then nail those and the uprights together to form the lattice.

topping off a green scene

right: Vine pole, fence, and screen in one, this triad of trellises supports climbing plants and provides playful shapes to pique visual interest. When stood together, the structures can form a corner screen.

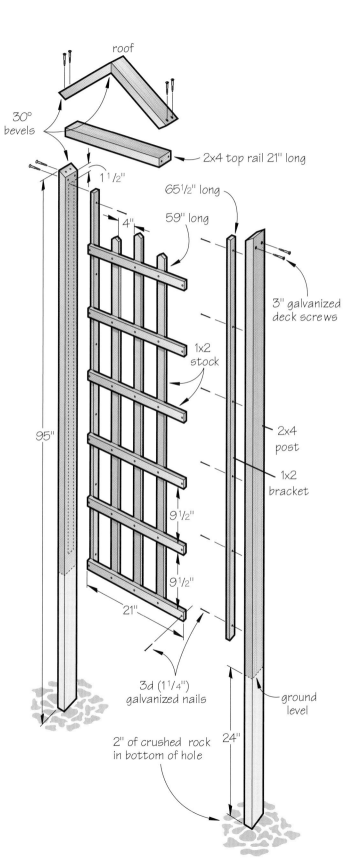

roof

30° bevels

2x4 top rail 21" long

1 1/2"

65 1/2" long

59" long

4"

3" galvanized deck screws

1x2 stock

95"

2x4 post

1x2 bracket

9 1/2"

9 1/2"

21"

3d (1 1/4") galvanized nails

ground level

2" of crushed rock in bottom of hole

24"

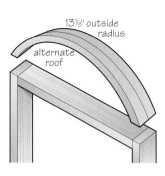

13 1/8" outside radius

alternate roof

Cut a 2×4 to make the top rail 21 inches long. Position the rail between the tops of the posts, and drive deck screws into countersunk pilot holes to secure it. Nail the lattice to the brackets. Finish by cutting the top pieces and screwing them into position.

Create the arched trellis top by cutting the post tops square as shown *at left*. Glue the 2×10s face-to-face. To draw the radius, use a piece of string tied between a pencil and a brad. Cut the radius using a saber saw.

Finish the trellises using exterior stain or sealer; or prime and paint them.

To anchor each trellis in the ground, dig two holes 26 inches deep for each post. Pour 2 inches of crushed rock into the bottom of each hole to provide drainage.

triple treasure

above: **Use cedar or pressure-treated lumber to make your trellis trio.**

containers

carried away

Garden containers are like the pumpkin in the Cinderella story that becomes an extraordinary vehicle. With a little paint or polish, any ordinary vessel gleaned from a garage sale, thrift shop, or junk pile could turn into magical transportation for your plants.

Transform pots, planters, boxes, baskets, wheelbarrows, wagons, or any containers that offer colorful charm into homes for plants. Situate a spectacular urn or other shapely vessel where it makes an outstanding contribution to the garden on its own. Use containers to decorate an entrance or brighten a corner. Choose vessels of weather-resistant materials that coordinate with the style of your house or garden.

ageless style

above right: A vintage watering can adds an elegant touch to a traditional garden.

paint buckets

right: Display color on a picket fence by painting galvanized French flower buckets with two coats of enamel paint. Drill a hole in the bottom of each bucket for drainage, and plant, or don't drill but fill with fresh cut flowers. Hang buckets on cup hooks.

rub-a-dub tub

above: A galvanized tub with awning stripes transforms a garden corner. Paint contrasting stripes in minutes or rub on a metallic finish to give the tub an aged look. Fill the container with ice and bottled drinks for a garden party.

magical mystery

left: A tall ceramic urn glows among the grasses. Its color is related to the encircling tapestry of greens but with just enough blue to stand out. The urn provides color and an architectural counterpoint to flowing grasses and shrubbery. Whether planted or chosen to make an artful statement on its own, a large, beautifully glazed container works magic in any garden.

accessories

fun with color

Garden ornaments add the finishing touches to your garden. Take advantage of the opportunity to express your personality as you integrate decorative elements with a focus on color.

Find garden ornaments among the everyday things stashed in your basement or garage, in salvage shops, or at yard sales. If the object of your desire is chipped, cracked, or faded, so much the better for its future life outdoors. A fresh coat of paint to highlight your garden's colors gives it a new life.

sunny side

right: **Work bird habitats into your color scheme. A bright yellow birdhouse glows in early-morning light. Birds won't appreciate the paint job, but you will.**

step-by-step art

left: Mosaic stepping-stones turn broken dishes into garden art. They're easily assembled with wet concrete and a round or square mold. Embed the mosaic design while the concrete is still wet.

pretty in pink

below: Plastic flamingos peek out of a patch of feathery ferns, enlivening the garden with their classic appeal. Gather a flock for the most impact and a little humor.

a patriotic scheme

you will need

- one 8-foot-long 2×2
- exterior paint (red, white, blue, gold)
- drill
- exterior-grade wood glue
- five flags on dowels/sticks
- 5-inch-diameter wooden ball (optional)
- jigsaw
- four 3-inch-diameter wooden stars
- five 2-inch-long-, ¼-inch-diameter dowels
- shovel
- concrete pre-mix (optional)
- ten 2-foot-long, ¼-inch-diameter dowels
- string
- red petunias, white vinca, and blue salvia

old glory garden

Based on an old custom of raising the liberty pole every Fourth of July, this flag pole garden waves the red, white, and blue at its top and bottom.

The patriotic planting of annuals echoes the flag colors in a star-shape bed. A blooming replica of the flag is more complicated but doable in a large area.

When planting, amass plants in groups of each color for best results. Use red, white, and blue petunias only, or choose alternative plants, such as verbena, pansy, ageratum (blue and white varieties); and red salvia, verbena, or dwarf snapdragon. Pluck and trim faded blossoms to keep the garden's color waving through the summer. Fertilize once a month.

For how-to instructions about garden projects go to **www.bhg.com/bkgardenprojects**

flowering tribute

right: **Red petunias, blue salvia, and white vinca echo the patriotic theme in a star-shape garden.**

1 assemble pole Make the (8-sided) pole by beveling the four edges of a 2×2. Paint the pole red, white, and blue. Six inches below the pole's top, drill four holes at angles to hold the flags. Embellish the pole with a gold ball at the top and white stars below, if desired. Paint the ball gold; let it dry. Drill ¼-inch holes in the ball's top and bottom and the pole's top. Glue and insert a 2-inch-long dowel into the ball's bottom; mount it in the pole's top. Insert a flag in the ball's top.

2 embellish Cut four 3-inch stars from wood, or buy precut stars from a crafts store and paint them white. Drill a ¼-inch hole in the side of each star. Glue and insert the end of the 2-inch dowels into each star. Repeat this process to attach each dowel to the pole. Dig a 2-foot-deep hole and set the flag pole in place. Refill the hole and firmly tamp the soil. Or anchor the pole in concrete, if you like.

3 stellar planting Arrange five stakes in a circle around the pole at points equidistant from the pole and one another. Place five more stakes in a smaller circle, at points in between the first circle of stakes, equidistant from the pole and one another. Use string to outline a star. Tie the string to an outer-circle stake, run it to an inner-circle stake, wrap it around the stake, run it to an outer-circle stake, and so on from stake to stake. Remove sod inside the outline; amend the soil. Plant annuals in a red, white, and blue pattern.

resources

mail–order nurseries, garden suppliers, artists/gardeners, and others

Burpee Co. (S, H)
300 Park Ave.
Warminster, PA 18974
800/333-5808
www.burpee.com

Forestfarm (P)
990 Tetherow Rd.
Williams, OR 97544-9599
541/846-7269
www.forestfarm.com

Gardener's Supply Co. (H)
128 Intervale Rd.
Burlington, VT 05401
888/833-1412
www.gardeners.com

Gardeners Eden (H)
17 Riverside St.
Nashua, NH 03062
800/822-9600
www.gardenerseden.com

Heirloom Roses (P)
24062 NE Riverside Dr.
St. Paul, OR 97137
503/538-1576
www.heirloomroses.com

Heronswood Nursery (P)
7530 NE 288th St.
Kingston, WA 98346
360/297-4172
www.heronswood.com

High Country Gardens (P, H)
2902 Rufina St.
Santa Fe, NM 87507-2929
800/925-9387
www.highcountrygardens.com

Hortico (P)
723 Robson Rd., RR #1
Waterdown, Ontario LOR 2H1
Canada
905/689-6984
www.hortico.com

Hydrangeas Plus (P)
P.O. Box 389
Aurora, OR 97002
866/433-7896
www.hydrangeasplus.com

Jackson & Perkins (P, H)
1 Rose Ln.
Medford, OR 97501
800/292-4769
www.jacksonandperkins.com

Kinsman Co. (H)
P.O. Box 428
Point Pleasant, PA 18950-0357
800/733-4146
www.kinsmangarden.com

Maryjo Koch (B)
555 Martin Rd.
Santa Cruz, CA 95060
831/425-7422
www.maryjokoch.com

Valerie Murray (B)
Abkhazi Garden
1964 Fairfield Rd.
Victoria, BC Canada
250/598-8096

Netherlands Flower Bulb Information
Center (B)
www.bulb.com

Karen Strohbeen (B)
The Perennial Gardener's Journal
http://www.pbs.org/perennialgardener

Proven Winners (P)
www.provenwinners.com

Safari Thatch and Bamboo (H)
2056 N. Dixie Hwy.
Fort Lauderdale, FL 33305
954/564-0059
www.safarithatch.com

John Scheepers, Inc. (P)
23 Tulip Dr.
Bantam, CT 06750
860/567-0838
www.johnscheepers.com

Sherwin-Williams Co. (H)
www.sherwin-williams.com/
DIY/exterior/default.asp

Smith & Hawken (H)
P.O. Box 431
Milwaukee, WI 53201-3336
800/940-1170
www.smithandhawken.com

Wayside Gardens (P)
1 Garden Ln.
Hodges, SC 29695-0001
800/845-1124
www.waysidegardens.com

Chris Keylock Williams (B)
6213 SE Main St.
Portland, OR 97215
503/233-7314

usda plant hardiness zone maps

These maps of climate zones can help you select plants for your garden that will survive a typical winter in your region. The United States Department of Agriculture (USDA) developed the map for North America, basing the zones on the lowest recorded temperatures. On a scale of 1 to 11, Zone 1 is the coldest area and Zone 11 is the warmest.

Plants are classified in zones by the coldest temperature they can endure. For example, plants hardy to Zone 6 survive where winter temperatures drop to –10° F. Those hardy to Zone 8 would die long before it's that cold. These plants may grow in colder regions but must be replaced each year. Plants rated for a range of hardiness zones can usually survive winter in the coldest region, as well as tolerate the summer heat of the warmest one.

To find your hardiness zone, note the approximate location of your community on the map; then match the color marking that area to the key.

Make sure your plants will flourish in the weather in your area. Consult the last spring frost map, the first autumn frost map, and detailed state-specific hardiness maps at **www.bhg.com/bkzonemaps**

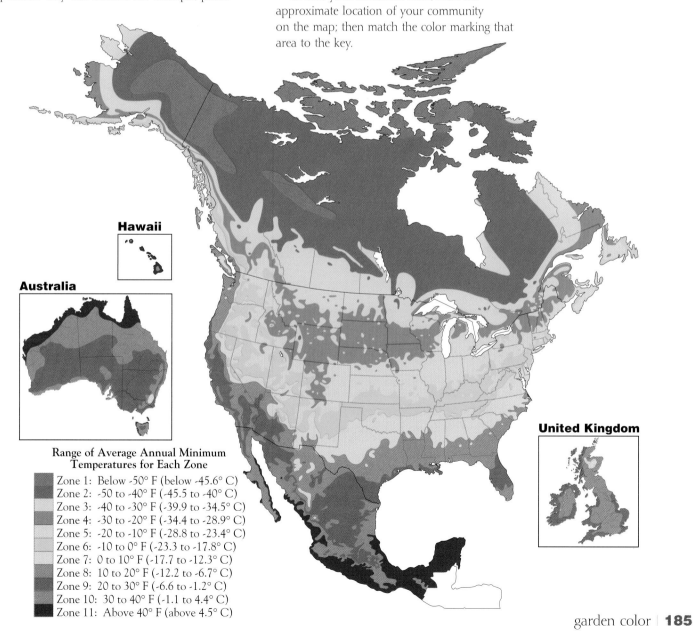

Hawaii

Australia

United Kingdom

Range of Average Annual Minimum Temperatures for Each Zone

Zone 1: Below -50° F (below -45.6° C)
Zone 2: -50 to -40° F (-45.5 to -40° C)
Zone 3: -40 to -30° F (-39.9 to -34.5° C)
Zone 4: -30 to -20° F (-34.4 to -28.9° C)
Zone 5: -20 to -10° F (-28.8 to -23.4° C)
Zone 6: -10 to 0° F (-23.3 to -17.8° C)
Zone 7: 0 to 10° F (-17.7 to -12.3° C)
Zone 8: 10 to 20° F (-12.2 to -6.7° C)
Zone 9: 20 to 30° F (-6.6 to -1.2° C)
Zone 10: 30 to 40° F (-1.1 to 4.4° C)
Zone 11: Above 40° F (above 4.5° C)

index

index

index

photo credits

Robin B. Cushman/PhotoGarden

43 (top left)

Sally Ferguson/Netherlands Flower Bulb Information Center

4, 6 (top right), 13 (bottom), 18 (bottom left), 34 (top) 82–83, 83

John Glover Cover

Mark Kane 51, 80 (bottom left), 150 (bottom)

David McDonald/PhotoGarden

18 (bottom right), 25 (top), 35 (top), 50 (bottom left), 50 (bottom right), 50 (top)

Clive Nichols 10 (top), 58

Cheryl R. Ritcher 12, 20 (bottom left), 36–37 (top), 37 (bottom), 124

Marilyn Stouffer 3

metric conversions

u.s. units to metric equivalents

to convert from	multiply by	to get
Inches	25.400	Millimeters
Inches	2.540	Centimeters
Feet	30.480	Centimeters
Feet	0.3048	Meters
Yards	0.9144	Meters
Square inches	6.4516	Square centimeters
Square feet	0.0929	Square meters
Square yards	0.8361	Square meters
Acres	0.4047	Hectares
Cubic inches	16.387	Cubic centimeters
Cubic feet	0.0283	Cubic meters
Cubic feet	28.316	Liters
Cubic yards	0.7646	Cubic meters
Cubic yards	764.550	Liters

metric units to u.s. equivalents

to convert from	multiply by	to get
Millimeters	0.0394	Inches
Centimeters	0.3937	Inches
Centimeters	0.0328	Feet
Meters	3.2808	Feet
Meters	1.0936	Yards
Square centimeters	0.1550	Square inches
Square meters	10.764	Square feet
Square meters	1.1960	Square yards
Hectares	2.4711	Acres
Cubic centimeters	0.0610	Cubic inches
Cubic meters	35.315	Cubic feet
Liters	0.0353	Cubic feet
Cubic meters	1.308	Cubic yards
Liters	0.0013	Cubic yards

To convert from degrees Celsius (C) to degrees Fahrenheit (F), multiply by ⁹⁄₅, then add 32.

To convert from degrees Fahrenheit (F) to degrees Celsius (C), first subtract 32, then multiply by ⁵⁄₉.